Pier Paolo Pasolini

Twayne's World Authors Series

Carlo Golino, Editor of Italian Literature

University of Massachusetts, Amherst

TWAS 657

LA CHIESA DI CASARSA
Sketch by Michael Dowd
College of Architecture, University of Washington

Pier Paolo Pasolini

By Pia Friedrich

University of Washington, Seattle

Twayne Publishers · Boston

Pier Paolo Pasolini

Pia Friedrich

Published by Twayne Publishers
A Division of G. K. Hall & Company
70 Lincoln Street
Boston, Massachusetts 02111

Book production by John Amburg
Book design by Barbara Anderson

Printed on permanent / durable acid-free paper and bound in The United States of America.

Library of Congress Cataloging in Publication Data

Friedrich, Pia.
Pier Paolo Pasolini.

(Twayne's world authors series; TWAS 657)
Bibliography: p. 140
Includes index.
1. Pasolini, Pier Paolo, 1922–1975—Criticism and interpretation. I. Title. II. Series.
PQ4835.A48Z686 858'.91409 82-945
ISBN 0-8057-6500-X AACR2

To "the dear and joyful" memory of my father, and to my husband.

Contents

About the Author

Born in Italy, Pia Cellerino Friedrich received her degree in Philosophy and Literature from the University of Torino. She has taught Spanish and Italian language and literature at the Italian College in Buenos Aires and the University of Washington, where she is presently an Associate Professor in the Department of Romance Languages, specializing in Italian literature of the twentieth century. She is the author of essays on Pier Paolo Pasolini, Cesare Pavese, Elsa Morante, and Alberto Moravia.

Preface

This book is intended as an approach to the works and the proposals of Pier Paolo Pasolini through a recognition of the ideological, political, and moral vicissitudes of the writer, followed (within the limits set by space and by linguistic and cultural barriers) by an analysis of the exemplary stylistic structures that, beyond the conditionings of psychological motivations, permitted the poet to express the metaphors of his destiny as a man.

Consequently, the initial chapters present the intellectual biography of the author. If it is difficult to take the bearings of one of the less tidy historical and critical situations to take shape around a contemporary author, it is however indispensable to investigate Pasolini's time, and with it the problems in which he was involved, the aspects of Italian culture he confronted and rejected, the various human, political, and social myths by which he was nourished.

The second part draws attention to the concrete dimension of those works that, in my judgment, show themselves to be specifically representative. They were chosen not to the exclusion of others, but because of precise considerations of a cultural nature: It is easily noted that several of Pasolini's writings—much more than others—impose intellectual references that are practically inaccessible to the nonspecialized or simply non-Italian reader. Reference has been made, however, to all the works published up to 1978, and they have been set within the biographical framework which, up to a certain point, conditioned them.

The outline used to frame the times and moods of Pasolini's works takes into consideration first of all the poet's adherence to Marxism and Communism. In dialectical Marxism Pasolini thought he recognized the correct method of research which, strengthened and deepened, would be capable not only of interpreting the world, but also of creating the conditions to change it.

The orthodoxy typical of many intellectuals of his generation was, however, alien to him, and the conflict that constitutes the fundamental core of his poetry would be fully manifested precisely in his personalization of ideology. At this point a preliminary observation is necessary regarding the absolutely privileged use—in the writings of Pier Paolo Pasolini—of synchysis, as a particular case of the general rhetorical figure of the oxymoron.

Despite the fact that it is a rather widespread phenomenon in poetics (from Shakespeare to the Imagists, from the baroque poets to the Hermetics), this dualism, this basic antinomy, never resolved but rather lived as an inspiring motive and as a poetic need, would be declared in his own case by Pasolini himself: passion *and* ideology. As such it is indicative of an entirely personal way of conceiving and especially of suffering a latent contradiction of values, expressed on all levels in that syntactic relation of antinomy which is, precisely, the synchysis.[1]

None of Pasolini's works is structurally and existentially exempt from it, but the roots of antinomy and its first, uncontainable explosion, are to be sought in the painful awareness of the clash between the suggestion of rationalist and Marxist humanism, and its political reality and realization. Innately free and nonconformist, Pasolini had the courage to recognize and come to grips with the difficulty (to say the least) of fulfilling the formulation of a humanistic hypothesis as a political endeavor, at least ten years before most Italian intellectuals. Certainly long before "self-criticism" appeared as a new type of conformism and its institutionalization finally acquired (as it is now acquiring, in 1979) all the characteristics of an intrinsic physiological phenomenon. And this is to Pasolini's honor. On the other hand, it cannot be said that he ever reached the rational moment of his rejection of allegiances, nor the precise definition of his political pessimism, first of all as human pessimism.

His refusal of the rational and historicist interpretation of reality and his consequent intellectual disengagement from within such a perspective was followed, between 1964 and 1965, by his encounter with psychoanalysis and its utilization, not as an "instrument" (that would have been too intellectualistic and captious for the poet's mental structure) but rather as an "occasion" and especially as a symbolic dimension. It is this connotation, this "cipher" that—neither analyzed nor schematized—would fill Pasolini's new works for theater and the cinema, first of all *Edipo Re* [Oedipus Rex], which evinces the flavor of the discovery of this new "scene." I would say ultimately that Pasolini, vis-à-vis psychoanalysis, does not espouse the theory but accepts its meaning (or suggestion, or contagion, as some—not at all contemptible—adversary of "psychoanalytic theory" might hold, given the fact that there remains to be explained the reasonableness of a perspective that ends with *Salò,* that is with the destruction of man).[2]

In the problematic encounter with the events of 1968, in itself determined by all the private and public experiences of the poet, one must recognize the final turn in Pasolini's itinerary. If the objectively regressive sign of the poet's hostility toward the student protest—especially in its first phase—was irrefutable, his later rethinking of that same contingency seemed to push him, in what would be his last years, toward an active, if contradictory, participation in the suggestions and changes of Italian reality.

On the whole, what is manifested in Pasolini's writings as discordant, disordered, at times incoherent, must be interpreted within the total significance of a human and intellectual figure for whom the synchysis functions as a permanent stylistic projection.

I have long reflected on the possible rendition of the word-concept *diversità,* which is fundamental in the entire context of the author's life and works: I have chosen the English term *diversity* because, notwithstanding its more immediate implication, it seems to capture the complex meaning of the Italian word that Pasolini himself had adopted to describe his psychological and social situation. *Difference* would be an inadequate term. "Diversità" for the poet meant not so much—or not only—homosexuality, as much as marginality. To be "different" meant, for him, being the social and psychological "negative" of others: the one on whom others unload and project the darker sides of their personalities.[3] His works would bear witness to this up to the end.

For all of us, his works bear witness especially to the Italian years from the Resistance to the time of terrorism. Through these intense, difficult years Pasolini took on the role of the active and at the same time passive interpreter of all those myths and ideologies that belonged to everyone but which in him, more than in any other, were lit up with a violently symbolic light.

Pia Friedrich

University of Washington, Seattle

Acknowledgments

The writers to whom I feel indebted are referred to in the text.

I want to express my sincere gratitude to my distinguished colleague and friend Antonio Pace, for his many valuable and considerate suggestions. I owe particular thanks to my Graduate Students who stimulated me to see things in Pasolini's works that I might well have missed. Gratitude is also extended to the Graduate School of the University of Washington for a Research Grant that helped me in the early stages of this endeavor.

Chronology

1922 Pier Paolo Pasolini born March 5 in Bologna.

1942 Publishes his first book, *Poesie a Casarsa.*

1943 Eight days after being drafted refuses to surrender to Germans and flees to Casarsa, his mother's home village in Friuli.

1944 Writes *I Turcs tal Friúl,* a historical play.

1945 His brother Guido dies as a partisan. Publishes *Poesie.* With close friends founds the "Academiuta di lenga Furlana" devoted to Friulian studies. Receives literature degree with a thesis on the poet Giovanni Pascoli. His father returns from war prison.

1947 Delivers his first political statement siding with striking day laborers of Friuli.

1949 Moves to Rome with his mother.

1954 Publishes *La meglio gioventù,* a collection of poems written from 1942 to 1952.

1955 Publishes *Ragazzi di vita,* a novel. Indicted for obscenity. With friends founds *Officina,* a literary review.

1956 Leaves the Communist party.

1957 Publishes *Le ceneri di Gramsci,* a collection of poems.

1958 Publishes *L'usignolo della chiesa cattolica,* a collection of poems.

1959 Publishes *Una vita violenta,* a novel. Father dies. *Officina* ceases publication.

1960 Publishes *Passione e ideologia,* a collection of essays, and *La poesia popolare italiana,* an anthology.

1961 Directs the film *Accattone,* whose script he had also written. Publishes *La religione del mio tempo,* a collection of poems.

1962 Publishes *Il sogno di una cosa,* a novel. Directs *Mamma Roma* and *La ricotta.*

1963 Is given four months' suspended sentence for *La ricotta.* Publishes *Il vantone,* a translation of Plautus's *Miles Gloriosus.*

1964 Publishes *Poesia in forma di rosa.* Directs *Il Vangelo secondo Matteo.*

1965 Publishes *Alì dagli occhi azzurri,* a collection of differently structured fictional pieces.

1966 Directs *Uccellacci e uccellini.* Assumes joint directorship of "Nuovi Argomenti," a literary review.

1967 Directs *Edipo Re.* Publishes *Pilade,* first theatric text.

1968 Directs *Teorema.* Publishes book by same title and *Manifesto per un nuovo teatro. Orgia* is presented.

1969 Directs *Porcile.* Publishes *Affabulazione,* a verse tragedy.

1970 Directs *Medea.*

1971 Publishes *Trasumanar e organizzar,* a collection of poems. Directs the *Decameron.*

1972 Publishes *Empirismo eretico,* a collection of essays. Directs *I racconti di Canterbury.*

1973 Publishes *Calderón,* a play. Directs *Il fiore delle Mille e una notte.*

1975 Publishes *La nuova gioventù,* a second version of a selection of his early poems; *Scritti corsari,* a collection of articles, reviews, and interviews, and *La Divina Mimesis,* fragments of a long planned prosaic interpretation of *The Divine Comedy.* Directs *Salò o le centoventi giornate di Sodoma.* Assassinated November 2.

Chapter One
Casarsa
The Roots

The pages that Pier Paolo Pasolini dedicates "to [my] new reader" in the preface to an anthology of his poetry[1] represent a partial but primary and explicit source for understanding the formative years of the author. These pages constitute the critically mature and synthesized version of two autobiographical insertions in an essay written in 1965.[2] Talking about himself, Pasolini interprets the beginning of his cultural development and existentialist constraints in a singularly objective way. A few letters recently published, written between 1940 and 1950 to various friends,[3] provide testimony just as revelatory, albeit occasionally naïve, sometimes characterized by predictive lyrical musings.

Pier Paolo Pasolini was born in Bologna on March 5, 1922. In October of that same year Fascism came to power in Italy and the country moved rapidly, if somehow obliviously, toward the totalitarian regime that was to end with World War II.

Because he turned into an ascerbic observer of Italian social and political life, particularly apt in touching the conscience of his contemporaries on an almost infinite number of moral issues, Pasolini's confrontation with his own "fascist" past may well appear surprisingly tame. When his statements are closely analyzed, however, his attitude confirms the ingrained honesty of an author who has never attempted to recreate for himself a political virginity. Very perceptible is Pasolini's effort to identify precisely both the moment of political awareness and the successive moment of his taking a stand.

As to his background, Pasolini dwells with suspiciously passionate insistence upon his "petit bourgeois" heritage. Nevertheless, when he tries to appraise his divergent roots, he incidentally and incongruously mentions his "paternal old noble family" from Romagna, but unmistakably identifies with his mother's peasant ancestry and with the land and people of Friuli. His choice is made and it will be one that will affect his emotional and intellectual life until his death and give depth and perspective to his whole work.

Pasolini, his mother, and his brother Guido, three years younger than he, moved frequently from one town to another, mostly within Northern Italy, following the peregrinations of his army officer father. Pasolini started writing poems at the age of seven, when he discovered, witnessing his mother's own attempts, that poetry could be "made" besides being read or recited. Thus his personality was in yet another sense molded by association with his mother. Meanwhile, Pasolini's father started placing high hopes on his son's literary career. Having learned to express himself by drawing before he was taught to read and write, young Pasolini would carefully illustrate his poems, yearning to become a painter.

Although later in life he would display a lasting disgust for the formal requirements of education and a transitory dislike for certain authors,[4] in secondary school Pasolini acquired a systematic training in studying and a keen sense of language. An episode that he considered significant (in fact, he repeatedly refers to it using the same words and placing it within the same perspective) is the reading of Rimbaud by one of his teachers at the Liceo Galvani in Bologna in 1937. For him, this reading constituted an intellectual discovery and, more significantly, the revelation of his political consciousness. Since Rimbaud and the Italian hermetic poets provided a cultural model rejected by the Fascists, Pasolini, then fifteen years old, discovered the core of repression. He himself defines his early opposition within cultural limits but, from what we can determine from his own statements, his anti-Fascism remained latent, and rather confused.

Political consciousness and literary beginnings

The author's cultural and in particular his literary perception, deepened and crystallized in the years between 1937 and 1941. With a group of friends who, like him, "wanted to be poets," Pasolini in 1941 worked toward the establishment of a magazine whose title *Eredi* [Heirs] indicates the position of its founders within the "new" Italian poetic tradition. Of this youthfully prolific and decisive period Pasolini has left us few and uncharacteristically detached accounts. Still, his letters remain to prove his position of "teacher of his contemporaries" and what Luciano Serra, in his lucid and intensely human introduction to the second group of letters, defines as "Pasolini's stirring vigor."

The first years of World War II do not appear to have left any definite impact on the author whose world seemed limited to the ancient maternal land of Friuli, which slowly took for him the guise of a mythical "expanse of space," untouched and privileged. To celebrate this world—his world and its life—Pasolini wrote, in the dialect of Friuli, *Poesie a Casarsa,* published in 1942 in Bologna at his own expense. Gianfranco Contini, a foremost literary critic, immediately expressed his favorable opinion of the book and promised a review; the young poet "jumps with joy, and dances under the arcades of Bologna." Contini's favorable review was not published in Italy. It appeared in the *Corriere del Ticino,* in Switzerland, because Rome, the overpowering "center" from which policies emanated, did not approve of dialects. (Neither did the poet's father.)

Pasolini's opposition to Fascism, which up to this point had been a cultural and intellectual necessity, became a matter of conscience and morality. The author's own attestations of this fundamental turning point in his development are scarce. Most relevant among them is an article that he published in March, 1943, during the Fascist regime, in *Il Setaccio* [The Sieve], a small review sponsored in Bologna by the Fascist party itself.[5] Entitled "Last Discourse on the Intellectuals," the article, with a naiveté more attributable to Pasolini's relative lack of an ideological base than to his youth, directs itself to the problem of the responsibility of the intellectual in wartime. In its pages, nevertheless, the author displays a fair level of cultural and ethical awareness and notable courage in stating the impossibility of reconciling the "trade" of the intellectual with that of the political propagandist.

Writing to his friend Serra toward the end of July, 1943 (after Mussolini's deposition), Pasolini had stated his revulsion toward war and the military service.[6] Ironically, he was drafted on September 1 of that same year. After one week, when the Armistice was signed with the Allies and the government newly formed in Southern Italy declared war on Germany. the improbable soldier deserted his outfit in German-occupied Livorno and fled to Casarsa, thus "performing" his first act of resistance.

In the months immediately before his conscription, Pasolini had been working on a thesis on coeval Italian painters. During the adventurous flight to Casarsa he lost all his notes. Subsequently he radically changed the subject of his study: from history of art to literature and from twentieth-century painters to the poet Giovanni Pascoli. If we keep in mind his reiterated declarations of esteem for Roberto Longhi who, at the University of Bologna, was the most respected among Pasolini's teachers and had inspired and supervised his thesis, and if we recall Pasolini's unfaltering interest in figurative expression, we cannot overlook the decisive significance of his shift.

Pasolini's choice should be ascribed to a consolidation of his new stands on culture and politics. He was among the first in his country to recognize Pascoli's function in renovating Italian poetic language. Although Pascoli's use of dialect was different from his own, in both intentions and results, Pasolini would attribute retrospectively to Pascoli the primordial inspiration for his linguistic solutions.[7] In addition, we cannot ignore Pasolini's interest in the thematic scheme of Pascoli's works and the vague populism that permeates them. Both thematic structure and populism find correspondence in the recent experience of *Poesie a Casarsa* and their emotional and intellectual substructure. Both, through a series of contradictions and re-elaborations, would condition a considerable part of Pasolini's work.

The political significance of his linguistic choice was further clarified with the founding by the poet and a group of friends, of the journal *Stroligut de cà da l'aga* in 1944. The title (Little almanac, this side of the river) specifies the symbolic and geographical limits of the community, and the articles included (Pasolini's in particular) reaffirmed the function and the vitality of the Friulian as a linguistic vehicle. The river is the Tagliamento and the land designated as "this side of the river" today forms the province of Pordenone. After a few issues the title was changed to *Stroligut,* extending the field of inquiry to the whole Friuli. Similarly, the inception of the "Academiuta di Lenga Furlana" at the beginning of 1945 shows the growth of Pasolini's and the other founders' motives in both cultural and ideological directions. With the support of substantial linguistic studies Friulian is accepted as a respectable language, while Friuli is projected as a culturally independent region.

Given the particular historical moment, immediately after World War II, the inescapable political consequence would be a movement (short-lived, in the case of Friuli, and never broadly assertive) toward political autonomy. Pasolini, in *Quaderno Romanzo,* a review of the "Academiuta," would argue cogently for independence.

The Resistance and the Party

One cannot disregard the fact that this moment of intense cultural activity in Pasolini's life coincided historically with the Resistance. Organized resistance in Italy had begun in the last part of 1943 as a reaction to the situation created by the Armistice, and it had developed the following year owing to the militancy of partisan brigades. The mountains of Friuli became one of the Northern Italian regions where rebel units were most active. Pasolini himself never became a partisan. His support, once again eminently intellectual and moral in nature, renounced immediate action. A letter addressed to Serra, written in May, 1944, is very explicit: "Alone I wander through the fields and I walk, walk in the empty, boundless Friuli. Everything stinks of gunshots, everything is nauseating if one thinks that upon this land those [people] are shitting. I'd like to spit on this land, stupid land continuing to bear green blades of grass and yellow and blue flowers, and buds on the alders. I'd like to spit on Mount Rest, far away on the edge of Friuli, on the Adriatic sea, invisible behind the Basse, . . . Everything reeks of bullets and feet. . . ."[8]

The intellectual interpretation of the Resistance as a total "political reality" would be expressed later in a poem in *La religione del mio tempo* [The religion of my time]: "Thus I came at the days of Resistance/ Knowing nothing of it but the style:/ it was a style all light, memorable/ awareness of sun. . . ."[9] Profoundly emblematic lines, but written in 1948 and the result of intellectual hindsight. Once again expressing the moral and human side of the political problem are the verses of "El Testament Coran."[10] Their protagonist is the slain young innocent partisan who is easily recognizable as Pasolini's brother Guido, killed at the beginning of 1945. The circumstances of this death, never clearly established in the official records of the Resistance, are described in detail by Pasolini in a letter to Serra[11] and then concealed by the poet in obvious reticence. Guido Pasolini had departed, not yet twenty years old, for the mountains, "with a gun hidden in a book," escorted to the train by his older brother to whom he was tied with strong bonds of affection and admiration. A member of the "Osoppo" Brigade of the Action Party, he was captured along with some comrades by a group of partisans from the Communist Garibaldi brigade, politically associated with Tito's fighters, and favorable to the annexation of Friuli to Yugoslavia. The whole group from the Osoppo was slain. Guido Pasolini, wounded, managed to escape and hide, but he was recaptured and killed.

Pasolini's painful silence on the death of his brother would be widely and shamefully manipulated by the rightist Italian press when the first details of the episode were revealed, along with the author's association with the P. C. I. (Italian Communist Party). The death of Guido was a profoundly traumatic experience that would leave in Pasolini's work a long train of anguished, and sometimes contradictory, themes for the attentive reader to identify and analyze.

An initial key for the interpretation of the symbol-theme of the "young-dead" running through Pasolini's poetry is a sentence from the previously mentioned letter to Serra: "Now all the love that boy had for me and for my friends, all his regard for us and for our beliefs (*for which he died*) torment me constantly." The contradiction "death by action" versus "beliefs" is clear, and it would weigh greatly on the P.C.I.conscience of the poet.

Pasolini's allegiance to the P. C. I. should also be placed against the background of this episode. Formally begun in 1947, this association provided the ideological tenets that guided his perceptions of the world until he died, despite his stormy and at times acrimonious rapport with the Party.

We have noted how the development of the Resistance coincides, within Pasolini's career, with his assumption of dialect as a political statement rather than an attestation of social awareness. In his steady program toward a definite political consciousness that could not exclude a genuine concern for the oppressed, Pasolini found himself surrounded by people whose archaic rites and archetypal language framed "his" ideal world, and who were living the Resistance as a revolutionary challenge. The Resistance had to be interpreted, in fact, not as a loosely patriotic, apolitical phenomenon, but as a driving force created and led by the political parties to bring about the end of oppression and war, and the beginning of a new social structure. The specific function of the Resistance as preparation for the revolutionary political process that would follow was embodied in the P. C. I. and the Garibaldi brigades that were under the control of the Party.

It is probably at this point that Pasolini, raised in a country with no cultural tradition of liberalism in the Anglo-American sense, chose the P. C. I., although he did not formally register until 1947. In his words, ". . . what made me become a Communist was the struggle of Friulian day laborers against the landlords, immediately after the war. . . . I sided with the day laborers. Then I read Marx and Gramsci."[12] The tenuous verses of "Le scoperta di Marx" [The discovery of Marx], the last section of *L'Usignolo della Chiesa cattolica* [The Nightingale of the Catholic Church], written in 1949 and published in 1955, recall this moment.

In reality, Pasolini's decision must not have been easy. His brother's death and its circumstances; his bond to his mother, which Guido's loss had complicated and intensified; the inevitable guilt feelings; the return of his father from war prison, depressed and ill, unable to comprehend and to accept the new social and political developments and even his son's literary activities and his stand in favor of dialect, all combined to make the years between 1945 and 1947 particularly trying and strenuous for the poet. His formal registration in the P. C. I. took place, then, in spite of everything and everyone. The reading of Gramsci, made possible by the political climate created by the end of the war in 1945, would constitute a fundamental experience that Pasolini himself would regard as a symbol of a contradiction never actually resolved. His longing for a popular reality existing outside of history, innocent and unaffected by the dynamics of change, clashed for the first time with the still-vague need for an ideological revision. At this point, in fact, Pasolini attributed to the peasant of Friuli a function of political and economic redemption that would situate within a framework of actuality the same world that until now had been an object of recognition and affection expressly because it did not portray the present.

The end of Casarsa

These were, in any case, the years during which Pasolini was actively a Communist. His political choice was reinforced by his work as a teacher which placed him in direct daily contact with the people. His performance as a teacher and as a political propagandist revealed Pasolini's strong pedagogical vocation. Both activities were abruptly interrupted in 1949 by the poet's expulsion from the school where he taught and from the Party.

In the previously cited introduction Luciano Serra writes: ". . . only then did we all become aware of his condition as 'a different one' . . ."[13] And a male colleague, like Pasolini a teacher in the school of Valvasone remarks: "Although living and working with him several hours a day, I never had any inkling of his leanings in this respect, even though he often talked of homosexuality in terms of normality, without considering it a form of reprehensible behavior."[14]

In a letter written at the beginning of 1950, after his flight from Casarsa to Rome, to Silvana Ottieri, a young woman who had been a very close friend during their university days in Bologna, Pasolini has left a human document of startling intensity:

> You want me to talk to you with honesty and constraint: I shall do so, Silvana, but in person. If it is possible to speak with constraint of a case like mine: perhaps I have done so, in part, in my poems. . . . I can only tell you that I shall continue to live the ambiguous life—as you say so well—that I lived in Casarsa, here in Rome. And if you think of the etymology of 'ambiguous,' you will see that he who lives a double life can only be ambiguous. . . . for many years I was what they call the consolation of parents, a model son, an ideal student. . . . This tradition of honesty and rectitude . . . has prevented me from accepting the verdict for a long time.[15]

The poet's admission of "perhaps" having spoken of this part of himself, which he had not yet been able to accept, in his poems, is for our purposes particularly important. In fact, reading numerous lyrics written in the years between 1943 and 1949 but published significantly much later in the *Suite Furlana* and in *L'Usignolo della Chiesa cattolica* we find direct testimony, even if subtly sublimated, of Pasolini's "diversity."[16]

The episode that cruelly exposes the diversity and, because of its political and human implications, would condition the entire existence of the man and the artist, occurred in October, 1949. As a result of action most probably taken against him by political adversaries, Pasolini was incriminated for "immoral acts involving juveniles." The facts of the case were never incontestably proven: The trial took place in 1952 and Pasolini was discharged for insufficient evidence. The occasion supposedly was a village celebration and a general and protracted bout of drinking. The young teacher did not deny that something had happened. But he tried desperately, though naively, to re-define the incident as an exotic literary experience, inspired by a recent reading of a novel by André Gide.

The expulsion from his teaching job could be taken for granted, in 1949, within the context of a small provincial town that until then had not known Pasolini's unorthodox sexual leanings. The expulsion from the P. C. I., on the other hand, when considered with hindsight after many years, betrays—more than anything else—the hasty reaction of the leaders who did not want the moral image of the party tarnished. The injustice of his Party, which had not hesitated to sacrifice him to an evanescent political motive, struck Pasolini as a violently "inhuman" act. This was the most significant among many manifestations of intolerance and rejection that characterized the troublesome relationships between the man, the artist, the critic, and the journalist on one side, and the P. C. I. It is only owing to moral consistency that a few days before his death Pasolini publicly declared himself to be "a Marxist who votes for the P. C. I."

Besides the reaction of his Party, the dismissal from his teaching post, which deprived him of any means of earning his livelihood, and the publicity which his case received at all levels, forced the poet to leave Casarsa and seek refuge in the anonymity of Rome, with his mother. Thereafter, every time Pasolini mentioned "the flight from Casarsa" he would neither be able nor try to hide his rankling bitterness toward the bourgeoisie. It is not improbable that the reaction to his homosexuality included the proletarian and peasant fringe, culturally conditioned, if for different reasons than the bourgeoisie, to condemn such behavior. Yet incapable of thinking that "the people," "his" people had judged and rejected him, Pasolini attributed to the middle class, especially the lower middle class into which he was born, the responsibility for some sort of betrayal in his regard. His attitude toward the P. C. I. would often be antagonistic and critical, but nevertheless sustained by the conviction of the historical necessity of the Party itself. The relationship with the middle class, in contrast, would never be restored. The poet himself, openly and repeatedly, confirmed the emotional and irrational nature of his hatred for the middle class. The hypothesis could be advanced that to the bourgeois clan of Casarsa and the world, Pasolini attributed the responsibility of having exposed his "sin" for petty political reasons. He also seemed aware that his Catholic and middle-class roots had imposed on him the repressive concept of homosexuality as repudiation of a moral order. Apropos of this point, we read in the previously quoted letter to Silvana Ottieri: "I have suffered what can be suffered, I have never accepted my sin, I have never come to terms with my nature, and I have not even gotten used to it. I was born to be satisfied, balanced and natural: my sexuality was over and above, it was outside, it had nothing to do with me. I have always seen it beside me as an enemy, I have never felt it inside myself. Only during this last year did I let myself go. . . ."[17] These words were written in 1950 but their implication has never been belied by Pasolini except, in part at least, in the film *The flower of the thousand and one nights* (1974) where homosexuality is seen and lived artlessly and serenely as an Eden reconquered.

In effect, the life of the man and his intellectual presence would be conditioned by the painful conscience of a guilty and predestined subjugation and by his constant attempts to rationally justify his "diversity." In the course of an inquiry conducted after the poet's death, which faced, among other problems, that of Pasolini's confrontation with his sexual reality, his cousin and friend Nico Naldini spoke perceptively of "honest dissimulation" within the family and, implicitly, by the artist. A more painfully bourgeois solution would have been difficult to reach. In any case there seems to be little doubt that from "the casual experience of his sexual diversity" Pasolini derived the impulse "to create for himself a situation of total diversity."[18]

Chapter Two
The Roman Years

The new environment: passion and ideology

The departure, or flight, from Casarsa to Rome in 1949 began a very difficult period during which Pasolini was, in his own words, "desperate, unemployed, the type that wind up killing themselves." The poet's father added his presence as a demanding invalid, tormented and unsympathetic, to a situation in which survival itself was problematical. Pasolini soon found a new circle of friends, and the author Giorgio Bassani was one of them. With their help the poet obtained a modest job as a teacher in a private school in Ciampino, and later, with the backing of Bassani, he began his contribution as a scriptwriter, his debut in the world of cinema.

In Rome the poet first lived in the urban part of the old ghetto, then moved to a suburban area populated then as now by immigrants from the South, near the Rebibbia penitentiary. These peregrinations represent uniformly extremely important biographical data, as decisive experiences which would be transfigured in the principal narrative and poetic works. In an interview released and published several years later Pasolini would stress: "In my narrative Rome has that fundamental importance . . . as a violent trauma and a violent burden of vitality; that is, an experience of *a* world and therefore, in a certain sense, of the world in general."[1] The studies on the ambience of the Roman masses which constitute the preliminary sketches for the two most significant novels and which would later be included in the volume *Alì dagli occhi azzurri* [Alì of the blue eyes] give us a precise sense of the importance that this encounter with the human and social realities of Rome took on for the poet. If the first notes written shortly after his arrival in Rome show a fascination with the masses of the inner city, the author's interest soon shifted to the outlying villages. There ever-growing numbers of a sub-proletariat nest, called forth by industrialization, was set apart both logistically and linguistically in a degrading environment. In this world of outcasts Pasolini glimpsed a unique culture whose members had well-defined principles, their own way of conceiving good and evil, and their own morality. They constituted for Pasolini a humane model of living opposed to the model presented by the bourgeois city. And, by an intellectual operation in a certain sense typical of Pasolini, the virginity of instincts and the primordial vitality that characterize this "different" people in their condition of ancestral misery, seem to be guaranteed by their alienation from history and society. *Pre-human, pre-rational, pre-Christian;* these are words that would come to be a part of the poet's vocabulary. They doubtless reflect his constant propensity to isolate, from among the phenomena deriving from the ineluctable situation of mobility to which the lower classes are subjected, their "endurance" (manifested both in customs and in outward attitudes) and various forms of sentiment, and to neglect the dynamics of the characters.

The first years in Rome constituted a problematical period in the life of the writer; a simple examination of dates will confirm its complexity and contradition. Inextricably involved in the historical context of postwar Italy, immersed in the "infernal" reality of the Roman slum, the poet was still not entirely detached from his Friulian sources and had not yet given up identifying himself with his subject, through the forms of popular epic. In the lines of "La meglio gioventù" (1949), the last composition in the collection of the same title [The Best Youth], Pasolini expatiates, still in dialect, on his expulsion from the Christian Eden of Casarsa, objectifying his vicissitudes in those of the other youths, constrained by some vague destiny to leave Friuli and to go into the world:

> . . . Come trains, take far away the youth
> to search the world for what at home was lost.
> Take, trains, throughout the world, dispersed from the land,
> these merry youths so they will laugh no more.[2]

The identification is still not so much political as existential, and the common experience is seen as a subjective conquest of maturity and of reality.

It is opportune at this point to remember the exact words with which the author specified the "moment" of his political choice, marked by his entry into the P.C.I. ("I sided with the day laborers. Then I read Marx and Gramsci." See Ch. 1, note 12). Pasolini's first novel is an attempt to elaborate that partial spiritual awakening. Written between 1948 and 1952 under the title *I giorni del Lodo De Gasperi* [The days of De Gasperi's reform], it was published in 1962 under the subtly emblematic title *Il sogno di una cosa* [The dream of something].[3] Alberto Asor Rosa writes about this work: "It is extremely significant to note that now (and only now) the country people begin to be introduced by him into an historical dimension in which suffering and injustice appear products not of nature but rather of oppression."[4] The historical and political motivations of the novel are in fact quite fragile and appear mainly in the last pages, while the constant dichotomy childhood-happiness-innocence/maturity-corruption-death is still bound to the symbols of Christian, rustic Friuli. The cultural orientation of the 1950s contributes in any case to confer a conscious critical stamp on the author's populism. The terms of poetic discourse are widened and, finally, ideological problems are faced.

In 1949 Pasolini also wrote the last section of *L'Usignolo della chiesa cattolica* [The Nightingale of the Catholic Church] entitled "La scoperta di Marx" [The discovery of Marx], which laboriously records, in Italian verse, the first perception of the historical values of socialism.

In his personal vision of the Roman sub-proletariat Pasolini discovers, however, a state of human authenticity which is first poetic, but also political and sociological. His interest in the objective conditions of the urban slums thus found its manifestation in that first populist resentment that had made him intuitively understand the collective drama of the peasant proletariat, also driven away from any participation in public matters. For the poet, beside that perpetual moment of contemplation and the absolutely non-historical discourse deriving from it, there appeared, a little at a time but ever more clearly, the other moment: that of the urge to make an ideological instrument of one's own art. Pasolini's personal history becomes emblematic of the agonizing contradiction in which a "traditional" intellectual—a poet—finds himself in trying to rationalize the lyric impulse of his individual "passion."

The embracing of Marxism and the reading of Antonio Gramsci can be recognized as determinant influences in the time-line of maturation which brought the poet to accept the necessity of a precise "ideology" as a cognitive impulse and as the consequent plan of action for the redemption of the lower classes. His recreation of the Friulian dialect had allowed Pasolini to express the innocent naturalness of a yearned-for pristine and unchanging existence. The short poems of "Le Ceneri di Gramsci" [The ashes of Gramsci], published in 1957 but written during the preceding years, use the Italian language and a whole new set of intellectual references to clarify the interior debate and to express the strength of a contradiction which in the heart of the poet would never be resolved. "Attracted by a proletarian life/ . . . my religion is its happiness, not its age-old struggle: its laughter, not its conscience" (1954).[5] Two years later, however, in another short poem Pasolini would write that "the world became subject/ no longer to mystery but to history."[6] From then on the poet would never refuse to confront history, but would always live this confrontation in the name of those who, like himself, are set apart and in a certain sense privileged because they are the unconscious bearers of truth and freedom. The objective critical dimension of the sociopolitical problem would never dominate the temperament, the "passion" of Pasolini. The author would never cease to put the populist sentiment based both in his nature and in his personal history before the ideological concept of "class"; his populism before scientific Marxism.

Humiliated and offended

Ragazzi di vita [Ragazzi], his first Roman "choral vignette" published in 1955, lies within this realm. As the lyric illustration of a world of down-trodden people who find a defense in physical and verbal violence against the inhibitions of nature and society, it is clear that the text is intentionally provoking. The reaction was immediate and controversial. While some reviews grasped the novelty of experimentation and the search that constitute the motivating nucleus of *Ragazzi di vita,* the criticism from the Communist side was largely negative. They complained of an excess of linguistic experimentation, artificiality, an absence of positive heroes, and, especially, a lack of "perspective."[7]

If the P.C.I. once again cast him out in an attempt to underscore the ethic propriety of its own organization and to reject the supposed ideological deviation of *Ragazzi di vita,* the Christian Democrats, the majority party in the government, were no more accepting of the work. They intervened heavily to persecute the author in the form of an accusation of obscenity against *Ragazzi di vita,* coming directly from the Premier. For the second time, then, Pasolini was caught up in an exemplary political game and his "public" judicial tribulations began. They would never end, even with his death, and he would be in the center of about thirty trials, besides the one at Casarsa. Not only would the author, in a bewildering series of appearances in court, have to explain again and again the motivations of his inspiration and the esthetic and expressive choices that followed, he would also have to defend himself against personal accusations, always subtly insidious, never definitely proven. Nearly all his films would be censored, denounced, and sued for crimes of obscenity, offenses against religion, and offenses against public morals.

The poet's militant commitment, matured during the decade from 1950 to 1960, was also defined through his collaboration on the review *Officina,* founded by Pasolini together with Francesco Leonetti and Roberto Roversi, friends from his university days. In the critical moment of the crisis of realism as the supreme expression of postwar Italian literature and of the crisis of Communist ideology (marked by the first revisionist urgings and by the "diaspora" of the intellectuals following 1956), Pasolini's presence in the arena of *Officina* was probative. His contributions always appeared to be connected—most of the time polemically—to the objective social and cultural climate of the 1950s and to his subjective situation. Taken together, such contributions elaborate the relationships between Italian literature and sociopolitical reality, the problems caused by the separation of literary Italian from the common language, and those of poetic and narrative technique as vehicles of a new reality. The last essays written for *Officina* clarify the essence of neo-experimentalism as "free" creative activity developed on precise humane and civil foundations, and the total proposal constitutes a useful introductory study of Pasolini's entire production.

The literary discourse of *Officina* was interrupted in 1959, following the publication of an epigram written by Pasolini on the death of Pope Pius XII: "You knew it, to sin does not mean to do wrong:/ not to do good, this is to sin/." Once again, in his penetrating moral reflection, in the search for his own "truth," Pasolini did not evade the din of scandal, nor the obstinate daily "battle." The polemic he opened on Pius XII's small love for the oppressed and the disinherited would have international repercussions. The death of Pasolini's father, which occurred during this period, took on the bitter form of the end of a nightmare: "He refused to take care of himself, in the name of his rhetorical life. . . . One night I returned home just in time to see him die."[8]

In 1959 Pasolini published *Un vita violenta* [A violent life], his second Roman "book," which clearly follows the outlines of a novel and respects the canons of socialist Realism much more than the first (*Ragazzi di vita*). The protagonist, Tommasino Puzzilli, is a "ragazzo di vita" whose human and political career is programmed between the dialectical poles of his initial conditioning (hooliganism and Fascism) and the apparent resolution of his entry into the Communist Party. However, even in this story of exemplary progressivism, there are insinuations of the favorite theme that contrasts childhood and adolescence as purity with maturity understood as corruption and death. In fact, death immediately follows the political redemption of Tommasino Puzzilli.

In 1961, shortly after the shutdown of *Officina* and the publication of *Una vita violenta,* at the same time as the cinematographic debut, the collection *La religione del mio tempo* [The religion of my time] appeared, presenting among other works some of the lyrics that had already been published in *Officina,* from 1955 onwards. In a note at the end of the book Pasolini stresses the necessity of reading *La religione del mio tempo* with due regard to the dates of the various pieces. In fact, if the protagonist remains the same—the intellectual formed in the political and moral climate of Italy after World War II—if his interest remains fixed on the "innocent" corruption of the sub-proletariat of the slums and on the crumbling city, there definitely appears, especially in the last compositions of the collection (whose dates Pasolini underlines) a retreat toward the themes and motives of the past, with respect to which the "historical present" assumes the function of analogic recall. The poet lives and expresses himself in an almost explicit abstention from direct political involvement. The tone of this renunciation becomes moralistic—"humiliated and offended"—in the face of corruption and the decadence of any authentic spirit of renewal in the moral and civil climate. Unexpectedly, Pasolini manifests an epigrammatic vein (as in the verses written after the death of Pius XII) which, aside from its novelty, is too often limited to the expression of a perplexing self-pity. For the first time, beside the name of Marx there arises that of Freud: "Vico, or Croce, or Freud sustains me,/ . . ./ Not Marx."[9]

Also for the first time, and this may constitute the ultimate significance of *La religione del mio tempo,* there appears the "African alternative." This is the only world with which "future history" can be identified because it is the only world unrelated to and remote from the bourgeois world: "And now . . . the desert, deafened/ by the wind, the splendid, foul/ sun of Africa, illuminating the world,/ Africa, my only/ alternative."[10] From now on Pasolini would invest the peoples of the Third World with those myths and symbols that would permit him to exorcise his personal sins and his guilt as a bourgeois intellectual, condemned to his inability to adhere without effort to the process of history.

The choice of cinema

In 1961, at the age of 39, Pasolini directed *Accattone* (*Accattone* is also the English title) following at least a dozen other films, a medium he had first essayed in 1954 with the friendly help of Giorgio Bassani. The narrative technique of the studies of the popular Roman milieu, later collected in *Alì dagli occhi azzurri,* was already consciously cinematographic. The figurative quality of some "scenes" of *Ragazzi di vita* and especially of *Una vita violenta* is evident, not to say obvious. *Mamma Roma* [Mother Rome], the second film entirely written and directed by Pasolini in 1962, is dedicated to Roberto Longhi, his teacher at the university, "to whom I am indebted for my figurative fulguration." In a long interview granted to Oswald Stack in 1968, Pasolini left us a series of fundamental notes, intended to illustrate his anything but chance "encounter" with the cinema:

. . . at first I thought the shift from literature to cinema involved simply a change of technique . . . [then] . . . I came to understand that the cinema is not a literary technique; it is a language of its own. . . . I came to the idea that the language of the cinema is not a national language, it is a language I like to define as "transnational." . . . So at first I thought it was a protest against my society. Then gradually I realized it was even more complicated than that: ... a passion for life, for reality, for physical, sexual, objectual, existential reality around me.[11]

And further:

I came to the conclusion that it is a non-conventional and non-symbolic language (*linguaggio*) unlike the written or spoken language (*lingua*), and it expresses reality not through symbols, but via reality itself.[12]

In such terms does the author-director stress an indistinct continuity between literary and cinematographic work and trace his interest in the cinematic experience back to its roots in his early cultural education. The cinema, moreover, responds to an expressive urge of the poet and narrator and, practically speaking, permits him to continue on the road of experimentation.

If, in addition, we consider the fundamental role assumed by Gramsci in the intellectual and political development of Pasolini, and his often-stated adherence to the Gramscian concept of "national popular culture," the cinematic experience appears necessary for still other reasons: While the author sees the literary message as destined to remain within the sphere of a traditionally educated and essentially bourgeois élite, the cinema offers him the immediate possibility of stirring up the conscience of a much larger public. For fifteen years, until his death and the heartrending testament of *Salò o le 120 giornate di Sodoma* [Salò or the 120 days of Sodom], the activity of Pasolini the director would be extremely intense and always intimately connected with the author's whole intellectual and ethical experience, as we can see in *Accattone*.

The children of the "marvelous and miserable city," lumpen-protagonists of our time, are inevitably the first protagonists of Pasolini's cinema. It would, however, be an error to identify, as many critics have done, the problematics of the parable of Vittorio called

Accattone with that of the exemplary story of Tommasino Puzzilli, the hero of *Una vita violenta.* In reality *Accattone* (like *La religione del mio tempo*) is largely extraneous to the programmatic intent of *Una vita violenta* in that it sacrifices all political dimensions to a protagonist who has regressed to a barbaric vitality and who is rooted in that irrational feeling for life corresponding exactly to the verses of *La religione del mio tempo:* "Our hope is equally obsessed:/ mine is artistic; theirs, anarchistic./ . . . both outside history/ in a world without outlets/ other than sex and heart;/ with no other depth beyond the sensual/ In which joy is joy, sorrow sorrow."[13]

Literary estrangement and "the third world" hypothesis

The Italian cultural scene during the 1960s was amply characterized by the activity of the Neo-avant-garde (defined by its break with the historical Avant-gardes of late Romantic extraction) as a phenomenon of total protest against the structures of the reality of that period and all their inherent expressive forms. In his reaction to this movement, which up to a certain point at least takes in the premises and the ideological instances of *Officina,* Pasolini (whose articles had vigorously stressed the need for new techniques of representation, composition, and literary meaning) assumed a heavily negative attitude. Beyond the partly justified and critically plausible charge of conceptual inconsistency on the part of the Neo-avant-garde and of its tendency to institute "the superstition of novelty," Pasolini scotched what might have remained a healthy exchange of opinions and methodological choices by accusing the Neo-avant-garde of trying to hold on to cultural "power" by reducing all protest against society to a protest against literature and finally against the verbal expression.

For our purposes it is not particularly important to analyze the substance and developments of a debate between two historically linked performances whose intellectual and moral testimony is certain. Rather, it is important to observe how, during this period and through the contingencies of this very debate, Pasolini openly, not to say publicly and at intervals clamorously, manifested a vigorous tendency to use his "diversity," condemning himself to estrangement. This tendency, of which we noted the first foreshadowings in *L'Usignolo della chiesa cattolica* and *La religione del mio tempo,* would gradually become more intransigent and would characterize the human presence of the poet and his behavior as a man of culture and of ideas up to the end.

In 1964 Pasolini published *Poesia in forma di rosa* [Poetry in form of a rose]. The components of this collection elaborate some of the themes of *La religione del mio tempo* and introduce others which constitute a not-always-rational development of the first work. An inflexible witness of his time, Pasolini captured the negative side of the precarious economic well-being that Italy entered into during the 1960s, which imposed on "his" sub-proletariat the consumerist and materialist vision of the petit bourgeoisie. What can be viewed as a phenomenon of considerable historical and social importance, namely the relative standardization of the masses, appeared to the poet in obsessively subjective terms: in his "diversity," which by now took on the character of an indisputable existential datum, he grew to miss the presence of those others who shared "diversity" with him. His function as prophet of a subordinate class was being taken away as that class was transformed. Therefore, the poet enlarged on a theme—already touched on in *La religione del mio tempo*—of a proletarian dimension comprising new scenes aad new outcast masses. This motif was at first limited to his personal vicissitudes: "And I seek alliances which have no other reason/ for being . . . than diversity, patience and impotent violence: the Jews . . . the Blacks . . . every banished humanity."[14] This obsession with subjective loneliness seems to be overcome in other poems. The myth of the Third World is defined, stretching splendidly "barbaric" unto the miserable villages of India and Guinea; promising, "red banners in the breeze," the paligenesis of Marxism, and the redemption of the world.

There remains to be considered the title of the collection, in which the ambiguously sexual symbol of the rose appears aligned with the thematic nucleus of several of the lyric poems. The provocative symbolism characterizing this text and, we must insist, its very title, confirms Pasolini's polemic tendency. It might also indicate the surfacing of a programmatic temptation and an obligation to "rationalize," to give form and logical evidence to a captious discourse (but a discourse bound to unequivocal suggestions and moments of reality), the deeper motivation of which is the personal drama.

In 1964 Pasolini presented, with a dedication "to the dear, joyful, familiar shade of John XXIII," the Pope who died in 1963, the film *Il Vangelo secondo Matteo* [The Gospel according to *St.* Matthew],[15] an attempt to historicize the essence of Catholicism. The poet criticizes Catholicism from a political viewpoint, and his reading of Matthew's Gospel obviously cannot be taken as a doctrinally orthodox work. The autobiographical component in the figure of Christ, radically "diverse" in that he is socially heretical, inflexible, and vehement, is evident. Equally evident is the attempt to draw from the crowds surrounding Christ the connotations of a primeval lack of corruption as opposed to the Pharisees and Sadducees who incarnate the metaphor of Power and those who hold and administer it. Far from being the work of militant or mainstream Catholic, this film is nevertheless a compendium of the intellectual ferment and those Christian Catholic exigencies recognizable in every work since *La nuova gioventù,* and in the very fact that Pasolini demonstrates a familiarity with the Gospels, notable in an Italian of this or any other time since the Council of Trent. The presence and the historical lesson of John XXIII (whose 1963 encyclical "Mater et magistra" had provoked enormous repercussions in Italy and the enthusiastic approval of the Left) is precisely acknowledged in the form and substance of the dedication of the *Vangelo,* and stressed by the poet in the interview with Stack quoted above: "But everything was made easier by the advent of Pope John XXIII who objectively revolutionized the situation. . . . The point is that I have contributed to the dialogue."[16]

Once again a participant in the historical scene, Pasolini interprets the crisis of religion, and the rebirth of faith, ecumenism, and the social involvement of religious consciousness.

The expressive instrument

Pasolini's discourse on "Nuove questioni linguistiche" [New linguistic questions], published in the periodical *Rinascita* in December, 1964, but previously disseminated in a series of lectures held in several Italian cities, once again brings to general attention one of the favorite themes of his critical research—the relationship between language and literature. The very style of the delivery, the openly polemic tone, and the content, involving a certain number of rather well known contemporary Italian authors, make one think that an impulse to rejoin the Italian literary scene is not entirely out of the question. This was in fact a moment characterized by intense theoretical discussion raised by the various groups of the Neo-avant-garde, when Pasolini's work was not only no longer a target, but seemed to be relegated to the literary past. On the other hand, the relevancy and the substance of the basic problems of language and literature are undeniable. The relationship between the writer and the expressive instrument within the sociological dimension of the evolution of the spoken language and in relation to a pragmatic knowledge of the world is a theme that Pasolini had discussed from the first years of *Officina*, in the light of the theoretical conclusions of stylistic criticism (especially according to the interpretations of Spitzer and Auerbach) and Marxism. The thesis advanced in "Nuove questioni linguistiche" is that of a supposed transformation of Italian from an essentially expressive language—conditioned by the literary element—into a preeminently communicative and rational language. The responsibility for this remarkable change would lie with the new neocapitalist, technocratic class, which possesses an effective economic and political power, permitting it to become the bearer of a given cultural and linguistic model. The axis of development of the new language (traditionally located in the central region between Florence and Rome) would now be moved to Northern Italy, site of the largest centers of technocratic power.

After the publication of "Nuove questioni linguistiche," the discussion and dispute over which became an integral part of the Italian cultural scene, came the publication of the essay "Il cinema di poesia" [The cinema of poetry][17] which proposes the theoretical elaboration of Pasolini the director on an international level. The essay analyzes the technical-stylistic tradition of recent development which, defined by the author as "poetical language," is opposed to the "prose language" of the traditional cinema. It consists of the "immersion" of the director in a character and of the adoption of the point of view of the character himself through an operation recreating with images the interior monologue of literature. The immense stylistic resources of the "cinema of poetry" in its successively "oneiric, barbaric, irregular, aggressive, visionary" dimensions clearly fascinate Pasolini and reconfirm his irrepressible experimental bent.

The film *Uccellacci e Uccellini* (released in the U.S.A. under the title *The Hawks and the sparrows,* 1965) signals the stylistic turning-point and, beyond this, constitutes the cinematic equivalent of Pasolini's moral quest. The action is set on the day after the funeral of the Communist leader Palmiro Togliatti, whose death is symbolically exploited to demonstrate the "decline of ideology" already witnessed in *La religione del mio tempo* and *Poesia in forma di rosa.* The film, structured as an expression of cinematographic "culture" more than as an expression of figurative interest, is not easy to interpret. To those who would later reproach him for having lost the fervor that had led him to create works in the national-popular style as inspired by Gramsci, and because of the fact that the masses were no longer the intended recipients of his message, Pasolini would say, paradoxically (and this became, more and more, a deeply rooted custom) but consistently with the speculative interest expressed in all his works during this period, with precise reference to *Uccellacci e Uccellini:*

> I have gotten away from my "Gramsci phase," because I was objectively no longer dealing with the world that Gramsci faced: What if the people for whom we must tell these national-popular stories no longer exist? At this point the common people and the bourgeoisie are jumbled into one single, identical mass. . . . I am therefore obliged, on the level of form, to make things that are neither probable nor plausible appear to be so. This forces me to use techniques in a different way.[18]

The films which followed (*Edipo Re, Teorema, Il Porcile,* and finally *Medea,* in 1969) are characterized by a stylistic unity which reflects the growing craftsmanlike care of Pasolini, the philologist of the cinema.

Alì of the blue eyes

In 1965 the poet published, in a volume entitled *Alì dagli occhi azzurri* [Alì of the blue eyes], twenty compositions of varying stylistic texture. The first go back to the Roman years, 1950–51; they are the painstaking studies Pasolini had written on the atmosphere of the slums, in his effort to understand and objectify their abject and innocent world, in preparation for the two major novels. The last compositions included are from 1965. In part stories, in part scenarios, some written in a mixture of prose and poetry, all scrupulously dated, conceived according to alternating narrative formulas which are clearly experimental, the pieces that make up this volume signal the phase of the poet's stylistic quest. It seems indubitable that the function of the book is to document the states of Pasolini's intellectual and ethical struggle, and the title is a further confirmation of the author's intent. "Alì of the blue eyes" is in fact the incarnation of a new hero. The Arab boy is the reconfirmed protagonist of a new history as the author had found him in his journeys through the countryside of Africa and the Middle East during the early 1960s, years which coincide with the emergence of the Third World in official history. Alì, who has already been introduced in *Poesia in forma di rosa,* primarily represents the sub-proletariat of the world, destined to replace the mythical "ragazzo di vita," whose poetic identity was being erased by a false process of acculturation.

The personal metaphor

The works and articles of the three-year period between 1967 and 1970 brought Pasolini into the center of louder and more heated public controversy. On the one hand, there were more and more episodes of violence (directed against the author), of intellectual dissension, of censure and near-persecution on the part of much of the press. On the other hand—and as a consequence—on the part of the poet there appeared an ever more urgent realization of his own existential reality and an obsession with his diversity.

The autobiographical imperative, always present in the poet's works as a contradictory and inescapable interior itinerary, became manifest in the tetralogy of *Edipo Re, Teorema, Porcile, Medea.* In 1967 with *Edipo Re,* Pasolini used the nonhistorical vehicle of the myth to set forth once again his persistent obsession. For the first time psychoanalysis becomes a concrete instrument of interpretation and of style. The personal metaphor is inserted in the classical myth of Oedipus as in a sort of dream-like wandering, the prologue and epilogue of which, emerging from the scenario of the poet's concrete memory, permit the revealing actualization and provide coordinates in space and time.

In their constant and coherent relation to the suffering and the passion of the poet, the two versions—literary and cinematic—of *Teorema* [Theorem, 1968] are related to *Edipo* as a further attempt at a metaphorical elaboration of diversity, but they are much more complex and ambitious than *Edipo*. The individual problem becomes exemplary, and psychoanalysis once again provides the cognitive instrument.

At this point Pasolini was evidently struck by the emergence of sex as an element of behavior and a paradigm of life. However, the prevarication of sexuality appeared to him not as a somewhat transitory evolution of conduct, but as the profound thrust of power immanent in the world. The deities of sex, for centuries obliterated and cursed, are now taking their revenge. One day their visible incarnation, their errant messiah, descends to earth to take possession of bodies and souls. This assumption is developed through a series of propositions which—in compliance with the title—fulfill an almost mathematical function. The hypothesis is that of the "religious" intrusion of a mysterious guest—successively defined as the Adorable, the Authentic, the Exterminator—into the circle of an emblematically bourgeois family. The autonomous literary text, which the author himself defines as a "parable," alternates the functional explanations typical of a script or an investigation with exquisite figurative evocations and poetic monologues of intense psychoanalytic connotation.

For the first time in Pasolini's literary and cinematic iter, the bourgeoisie becomes the protagonist, and his categorical judgment against it is also the denunciation of another aspect of the existential drama of the author: the fact of being bourgeois and of bourgeois lineage, and of knowing that the bourgeoisie has finished its historical mission and has "replaced the soul with the conscience."

In the context of the poet's often-stated aversion to the bourgeoisie, we should place the poem-pamphlet "Il PCI ai giovani" [The PCI for young people], which appeared in the weekly *L'Espresso* of June 16, 1968.[19] It is not only contemporary with *Teorema,* but it is also clearly complementary to one of the poetic passages of the book. Pasolini writes, in white heat and to the point, to stigmatize the death of a young policeman by the hand of the student protesters of '68 in Rome.

The polemic substance of the "pamphlet" is established in the proclamation of the irreversible dichotomy between student-bourgeois and policeman-son-of-the-people, which symbolizes for the poet the absence of any historical or moral validity in the student movement and its struggles. Aside from their immediate provocatory intention, the verses of "Il PCI ai giovani," as well as the "Apologia" which Pasolini published as an explanation of his own "ars rhetorica," and other writings of the same or immediately succeeding period, present a rather interesting schematic description of the ideological (or nonideological) core of the Italian—and by extension, European—student movements of 1968. Pasolini makes a distinction between "protest" and "revolution," defining the first as "ontological" and "psychological," the second as "philosophical" and "objective." For a revolution to occur, objective circumstances must exist which our time (and this is the link with the obsessive personal vision of the author) has destroyed. In a homologized society in which the bourgeoisie is becoming the sole human condition, for Pasolini the movements of '68 constitute only a phenomenon inherent in the system, where the bourgeois children, symbolically dressed according to the consumerist canons, rebel against their bourgeois parents.

The real drama of Pasolini, as it was developing and shaping itself during these years, thus had its roots first in the disappearance of the mythical sub-proletariat world (and with it, the disappearance of the only possibility for a revolt against the bourgeoisie) as the symbol of innocence and youth. The generation gap, which Pasolini intuited in its historical implications, came to be lived by him in human and, as always, painfully personal terms.

Il Porcile [The Pigsty], produced in 1960, once again denounces the neocapitalist society—of which the pigsty is the metaphor—and the repression of the "diverse." Furthermore, the motif of the ancestral conflict between father and son is reaffirmed and elaborated upon. This is one of the most complex and certainly one of the least understood of the films directed by Pasolini. Its interest seems mainly cultural: Psychoanalysis (and almost certainly Freud's essay "Totem and taboo") is our first key to the work, and reveals the link with

Teorema and the author's progressive estrangement from ideology. Cannibalism, with all its possible symbolic interpretations, is in fact presented (like the pansexualism of *Teorema*) in the function of palingenesis: The break with Marxism could not be more evident nor more absolute.

In 1966, during a period when illness had forced him to be physically inactive for a time, Pasolini's interest had returned to the theater, a literary genre he had ignored since the drafting of a youthful work, *I Turcs tal Friúl,* written at Casarsa in 1944. The return to the theater constituted for the poet a formal return to "literature," since the six works composed in 1964 were written in verse, a genre which Pasolini, wrapped up in his interest in the cinema and in his more immediate task of writing essays, had abandoned for years.[20] The reasons for the change appear as always to be numerous and contrasting. It is interesting to note that in that same year, 1966, the poet had assumed the co-direction of the specifically literary review, *Nuovi argomenti.*

The choice of the theater is in any case coherent with the indomitable critical and moral attitude of Pasolini; the strain and decay to which both narrative literary production and the cinema are inevitably subject because of the rampant industry of the culture did not escape him.

That the theater appeared to the poet as an expressive form permitting a direct and sincere communication with the public is clearly indicated in the *Manifesto per un nuovo teatro* [Manifesto for a new theater] published in *Nuovi argomenti* in 1968. There Pasolini proposed a scenic function which, beyond the experiences of the traditional function, restores to the *word,* in its total and charismatic meaning, the role of vehicle of thought. The *Manifesto,* a sort of guideline for the celebration of a rite that could renew the meanings of the Athenian Greek theater as a cultural form of political experience, is at times openly polemic, but substantially aligned with Pasolini's speculative heterodoxy. The prospective of a new theater as a happening "with all rules suspended" reaffirms the author's willingness to accept the suggestions of the literary climate of the time. It is important to note that—beyond a purely cultural connection—the adoption of a structure "with all rules suspended" reveals a growing diffidence toward any cognitive experience of the Marxist type. It also implies—with the rejection of any easily pragmatic interpretation—the possibility of translating consciousness-raising into speculative terms and favors a revaluation of the irrational level. It is significant that most of the texts that Pasolini wrote for the theater in 1966—from *Orgia* to *Pilade* and *Affabulazione*—are substantially a restatement of the theme of diversity in the political and social sense, in an openly autobiographical framework.

Of all these works, *Affabulazione* [Affabulation] seems to me the most significant as text and interpretation of Pasolini's conception of that central, and for him painful, point, the father-son relationship: a determining reality which, at a certain moment in his life, the author could no longer evade. The style bears the imprint of Greek tragedy and the general approach is ingenuously anti-Freudian. The play, a rather mature elaboration of homosexuality as a metaphysical paternity, centers on the impossibility of an Oedipal relationship between father and son, an impossibility inexorably leading to the almost ritual killing of the son. Bearing in mind that, as is stated in the text, this impossibility always leads to a killing—there is no alternative—usually it is the fathers who kill their sons. From time to time, however, the author states—and it is not easy to draw one's mind away from the fascinating prophetic touch—it is the son who manages to kill the father. The anti-Oedipal solution of the play is eloquent. On the other hand, what is to be done with "an unknown father," about whom it is nevertheless necessary "not to be silent" (as in "Timor di me?" in *Trasumanar e organizzar*), if not to reinvent for him, obscurely, an archaic role as "devourer of the son"?

Medea (1969), Pasolini's tenth film, was inspired, according to the poet, by recent reading in the fields of history of religion and ethnology. If James G. Frazer, Mircea Eliade, and even Claude Lévi-Strauss provide the general cultural context and the inspiration for the background of the film, the ideological source is still that of the yearning for an archaic universe whose severe protagonist Medea, the repository of all positive values, confronts the heavily rational, pragmatic intrusion of Jason. The drama thus shows the uncompromising encounter of two cultures and two civilizations. The fabled quest for the golden fleece loses all its mythical splendor to assume the character of a space science-fiction episode. (Once again we must compare dates: the "conquest" of the moon came just before the film.) The metaphor of a utopian, innocent, Third World in contact and in conflict with the rapacious Western civilization is suggestive.

Something that no longer exists

In number 201 of *Cinema nuovo* (Sept.-Oct., 1969) Pasolini posed the question of "how one can oppose cinema as the 'medium' of mass culture."[21] The author answered his own question with obstinate disenchantment: "By making an aristocratic cinema; *inconsumable.*"[22] *Medea* also constitutes the exemplary projection of this inexorable necessity.

The three films which followed—*Il Decameron* [The Decameron, 1971], *I Racconti di Canterbury* [Canterbury Tales, 1972], and *Il Fiore della Mille e una notte* [The Flower of the Thousand and One Nights, 1974] were grouped by the director himself into the "trilogy of life" and signal another phase of relative transition. Submitting as always to contrasting ideological tensions, Pasolini gives us a dispirited explanation of what, at least at first glance, might seem to be the happy breakthrough of the *Decameron.* At the same time he sets forth the premises of an attitude which would lead inevitably to the absolute intellectual solitude of his last years:

> The great desire to laugh [in the *Decameron*] comes from the final abandonment of "hope," which is and always has been solely rhetorical in any case. For all practical and ideological purposes, I have lost *all hope.* This "hope" of Marxist praxis and bourgeois pragmatics—where does it come from? It comes from a common source—Hegel. I am *against Hegel.* . . . Thesis? Antithesis? Synthesis? It seems much too easy to me. There are only oppositions, irreconcilable oppositions. Therefore, no "bright future," no "better world." . . . Finally, living like the birds of the air and the lilies of the field, taking no thought for the morrow (which is not a synthesis, but another opposition), I enjoy a bit of life and liberty. . . . So my attitude toward reality is "cruelly hedonistic," yes; and in fact, in the *Decameron,* which I am now finishing, the narration is ontological: we tell tales for the joy of it, or act for the joy of acting. What is being told and acted? Something that no longer exists: people, feelings, things.[23]

Inspired by eight of Boccaccio's hundred stories, vaguely set somewhere around Naples, *Il Decameron* seems to be without all the historical and social components of the literary work after which it is named. The ideologies and problems that up to now engaged his expressive force apparently disappeared from Pasolini's horizon. The poet describes carnal love without dramatics, and during the production of the film he proclaims to anyone who will listen: "I am living my moment of joy."

Beyond any technical or stylistic reflections and aside from the novelty of the director's "game," we must, however, note that Pasolini's most significant choice (and therefore the trait that characterizes his argument in the *Decameron*) is that of Ser Ciappelletto, of whose "diversity" Boccaccio himself has informed us. In the structural organization of the film this character becomes the symbol of irrepressible human passions.

The next film, derived from the *Canterbury Tales,* presents an analogous selection of emblematic cases set by the director in an existential context whose luxuriant sensuality should have the power to redeem man's life from the weight of cultural stratification. However (and here is the important disparity with respect to the *Decameron*), life and sex seem to have lost all their joyful exuberance. The episode of greatest stylistic prominence (practically reinvented by Pasolini) is that of the blackmail of the sodomites. Rather more bitter than funny, the event seems to be filtered through the cold, cruel vision of the informer. The sense of guilt is heartrending: What in the *Decameron* were "free" bodies, drawn in a happy and open historical dimension, now appear to us literally goaded by demons of the most terrifying medieval Catholic tradition.

Il fiore delle mille e una notte (1974) obviously concludes the discourse initiated with the *Decameron* with one of the richest metaphors ever devised by Pasolini. Its complex elaboration permits the repetition of an emblematic episode, the characters of which live again, by an analogical continuity, some within the others. Homosexuality, finally represented with absolute and unabashed sympathy, becomes the object of a polemic hyperbole which assigns it the primary responsibility for "Eden-like" regeneration. Since, according to Pasolini's personal vision, the innocent affirmation of the biological motives of existence can now take place only among "rediscovered" people, in a universe before history and in an indefinite space, the protagonists, all endowed with a smiling youthful beauty, move in a world without precise geographic coordinates, where the horrifying phantasms of anthropological mutation caused by the consumer ethic have not yet made their mark. In my opinion it is precisely this emphasized isolation from history that defines the ultimate meaning of the "trilogy of life" as the impossible search for authentic values in a degraded world.

In 1971 Pasolini published *Trasumanar e organizzar* [Transhumanize and organize], a volume of poetry. Some of the poems had appeared in *Nuovi Argomenti;* not all are precisely dated, but most were written after 1968. The continuous and calculated superposition/juxtaposition of private history and external history, and the inextricable interdependence of one on the other, seem to constitute the overall statement of the collection. The title, alluded to by the poet himself in the interview with Duflot,[24] is tellingly ambiguous. *Trasumanar* (the apocope of the verbal infinitive goes back to Dante), that is, the transhumanization which signifies spiritual ascent, represents the other side of *organizzar,* which should be understood as institutionalization. Between these two dialectical poles, presented in a key of alternating bitter sarcasm and heartbroken realization, we find the thematic points that constitute the nucleus of all the works of the later years. It is opportune to note at this point that what might seem a "monodrama" on the part of Pasolini, characterized by the sometimes obsessive repetition of motifs, is in fact filtered through a complete human and moral experience. In this, as in the other collections and in all the "curriculum" of the author, the writings always "testify," if not to one point of arrival, at least to a succession of points.

Pasolini's stubborn impulse to protest and argue continues to invoke a recuperation of rational and moral order. The polemic against the P.C.I. reechoes in tones of exasperated animosity in the poem "Trasumanar e organizzar," the title of which indicates its centrality. The not-always-rational total rejection of the bourgeoisie is reaffirmed and extended. There is more and more ardent self-defense and equally ardent self-accusal. The generic adhesion to the sub-proletariat includes new segments of the world and of humanity, such as Eritrea and Brazil. The theme of youth protest, of great importance to the poet because of all the personal implications involved, re-emerges as the irrationality of unconsciously bourgeois children exploited by their consciously bourgeois parents.

The most conclusive pieces in *Trasumanar e organizzar,* however, are those expressing a sorrowful awareness of an inability to assume a precise role in the confused dynamics of contemporary reality and to find even an approximate political definition and corresponding practical choices. In the general context of a collection in which the prevalent form is free verse, sometimes tending toward the tiredly prosaic, the problematic elaboration of these pieces is sustained by metric structures and complex and tightly controlled stylistic figures.

In *Trasumanar e organizzar* we find at last the first published examples of an "explicit" elaboration, in poetry, of the painfully autobiographical theme of paternal relationship and rejection: "The father is there, yes, he! Do you think that I know him? . . . You smile at the Father/ that person about whom I have no information,/ whom I have frequented in a dream which evidently I can't remember/ . . . ."[25] The paternal image is "quoted" with a detachment whose cold irony prolongs the original anguish and the subsequent sense of lack and loss.

The poem "La restaurazione di sinistra" [Restoration from the left], the central piece of the section that bears the same title, reveals the ideological nexus between *Trasumanar e organizzar* and *Calderón,* a tragedy in verse published in 1973 and staged only recently (May, 1978). The play, divided into sixteen episodes and three stasima in the form of Greek tragedy, reveals a stylistic consistency with the proposals of the *Manifesto per un nuovo teatro.* Calderón de la Barca, the Spanish dramatist who wrote *La vida es sueño,* is the cultural and polemic pretext permitting Pasolini to present an episode hinging on the ambiguous and unresolved alternation of dream and reality, following a scheme of analogical repetition very much like the structure of *Il Fiore delle mille e una notte.* The protagonist, Rosaura, lives and dreams—or dreams—a life as an aristocrat and a poverty-stricken life, without being able to recognize herself in either, until her "definitive" awakening in her real identity as María Rosa, the middle-class wife of the eternal, emblematic Basilio, who is the incarnation of "sanity." Basilio has the task of explaining to María

Rosa (alienated and aphasic in an unconscious attempt not to remember her dreams in order not to have to tell about them) that the only dream she spontaneously "remembers"—the one about the epic liberation from the prison camp by an army as large as the sea, made up of singing workers with black overalls and red flags and red kerchiefs around their necks—is the only real "beautiful dream. . . . Because everything you dream, past or future/ might someday come true. But as for this one about the workers, there is no doubt:/ this is a dream, nothing more than a dream."[26]

And here is the essence of "the real tragedy," the realization of absolute power, which not only has complete totalitarian control of present reality but invades even the dreams of the future. The sinuous elegance of *Calderón* is the most intense moment of Pasolini's pessimism. María Rosa is destined to recognize herself for what she is, and to enter again into reality and reason . . . in May, 1968.

Pablo, son and lover, beloved and hated, is one of the protagonists of the "wasted" year 1968. The ideological structure governing this work is once again a deeper, lucid, and very personal interpretation of the events of '68: "Power, which had always/ recreated itself/ in its own image,/ recreated itself this time in a different form."[27]

Beyond the subtly personal motives of a first level of opposition, Pasolini goes on to intuit the inner drive for authority—and thus for symbolic "paternity"—on the part of the rebellious children who "reject all fathers" and, through this absolute repudiation, give life to a new political absolute, already foreseen and described by the poet in the difficult verses of "La restaurazione di sinistra."[28]

Corsari writings

In his unremitting effort to describe the motivation of his own poetics in all its forms and to illustrate the development of his many critical, theoretical, and political interests, Pier Paolo Pasolini has left quite a number of articles and essays. I have already remarked that *Passione e Ideologia* (1960)—the first of the three volumes of essays edited by the author—possesses all the characteristics of a propaedeutic for the interpretation of an historical and cultural period.

The second collection, published in 1972, is entitled *Empirismo eretico* [Heretical empiricism].[29] It contains studies and articles written at different times (after 1964), on many different subjects. Divided into three sections dedicated respectively to Language, Literature, and Cinema, the volume includes writings of notable historical and critical importance such as "Nuove questioni linguistiche," "Intervento sul discorso libero indiretto," and the "Apologia" which explains the intent of the too-famous poem, "Il PCI ai giovani." I have referred to these studies and others in the same collection and shall have occasion to refer to them again.

In this volume the author's horizon is greatly expanded to include the crucial writings of Claude Lévi-Strauss, Roman Jakobson, Roland Barthes, Lucien Goldmann, and even George P. Murdock and Vogt. In this sense, *Empirismo eretico* shows the consistent development of premises established in the second part of *Passione e Ideologia,* where Pasolini went from the lesson of Antonio Gramsci to that of György Luckács and then attempted to adopt the critical tools indicated by Erich Auerbach, Leo Spitzer, and Ernst R. Curtius, at that time relatively novel in Italy.

Once again it would be futile to search among the pages written by Pasolini for absolute philological rigor, patient verification, or total critical and logical consistency. We find instead flashes of prophetic genius, great intelligence in reading, and a persistent inability to separate the function of the critic from that of the witness.

The latter characteristic, whether positive or negative, constitutes the link between *Empirismo eretico* and the last book of essays edited by Pasolini himself. The publication date of *Scritti corsari* [Corsari writings] is November 6, 1975, four days after the poet's death.

Empirismo eretico had been greeted by the critics with almost complete indifference. Nor had *Trasumanar e organizzar* or *Calderón* inspired great interest or understanding. The voice of the poet seems lost in a void. Voluntarily cut off from literary society, Pasolini set himself up as an essentially truthful witness and judge of the situation in Italy at the time, which appeared monstrous to him.

Many of the documents of his last years (which had originally appeared in various Italian dailies and weeklies, especially in the *Corriere della sera*) are gathered in *Scritti corsari,* a volume consisting of twenty-five articles written between May, 1973, and February,

1975, plus several "documents and enclosures." The specific themes coincide only minimally with those of the two preceding volumes of essays. There are a few short, as always lucid and aggressive, "interventions" dealing with literary criticism or general cultural themes, but the thrust of *Scritti corsari* is essentially socio-anthropological and political. The "mood" of the pieces is, for the most part, visceral and contradictory. The stands he takes (against divorce, against abortion, against permissiveness, against pseudo-progress leading to uniformity) seem at times to lend cultural dignity to dangerously conservative attitudes.

And yet, beyond the evident—and often puzzling—one-sidedness of the paradoxes of Pasolini's argument it is possible to single out the moral sense of his indictment, intended above all to criticize "false" economic development, which is paid for, in the eyes of the poet, by an irreparable loss of humanity, and the general tendency to accept without protest the political and economic trappings of the consumeristic "new Power," conceived as "development without progress."

Furthermore, in *Scritti corsari* Pasolini returns inevitably to a theme that had aroused his interest and commitment since his youth in Casarsa, when he had tried to escape the climate of Fascist conformism, confronting for the first time his responsibility as an intellectual. In the decisive, if not logically worked out, essay entitled "Il romanzo delle stragi" [The story of the slaughters],[30] dated November 14, 1975, Pasolini clarifies the essentially "cognitive" role of the intellectual, who is in a position to interpret rationally, and to give unity and coherence to, the fragmentary character of reality. Since, on the other hand, he feels the full weight of the isolation inherent in such a role in a society that conceives literature uniquely as a "pretext," or a "spiritual guide," or a "paradigm of inner freedom," the poet debates whether the intellectual should and can remain autonomous, or whether he should involve himself in political activity. Pasolini conceives the relationship between politics and culture as conflict in which freedom—or autonomy—of the intellect is opposed to concrete political involvement. Once again the poet is trying to resolve, within his role, "his" position between culture and politics, which he translates, once again, in terms of passion and ideology.

The new youth

Also in 1975, Pasolini published *La nuova gioventù* [The new youth], a volume including the first group of the Friulian poems, *La meglio gioventù,* dated between 1941 and 1953, and introducing a second version of two sections of that work, *Poesie a Casarsa* and *Suite furlana.* Comprised in the same collection are several "Italo-Friulian" pieces written between 1973 and 1974.

The poet takes the verses written twenty-five or thirty years before and rewrites them under the same titles, using the same metrical structures. *La nuova gioventù* is the result of a genial poetic operation, perfectly consistent with Pasolini's speculation, which was leading at that time to *Scritti corsari;* and, in a sense, it sums up the experience. In several of these essays the poet had developed and stressed the concept of acculturation—shaped and controlled by the mass media and its alienated and alienating messages—as the agent responsible for the destruction of a vast number of real, humanly exemplary cultures. In the rewriting of *Poesie a Casarsa* and particularly in "Vilota," in place of one of the many celebrations of the green fields of the Friuli, we find the cry that in those fields "something human has ended!"[31]

Along the same lines, with greater or lesser lyrical success, the poetic settings characteristic of the youthful years are now put into a framework of unreachable remoteness, and the images are systematically desecrated. Hope is replaced by disillusionment and the lively and tender Friulian countryside gives way to gloomy "scenarios" tossed in the wind; enchantment is succeeded by the most desolate disenchantment. David, perhaps the dearest of the recurring human images—poor, young, and uncorrupted—is now only the "fertilizer" which nourishes dreams.

Closest to the ideology and polemics of *Scritti corsari* is the last section of *La nuova gioventù,* entitled "Dismal enthusiasm." Here Italian alternates with dialect and at times, in the effort to recreate an historically plausible spoken language, contaminates it. In these last compositions, however, we can glimpse a certain innovative break in the laborious attempts to find and propose an antagonistic solution. These are attempts not so much to negate painful regressive recourses as to overcome them: "I look back, and weep/ for the poor towns, the clouds and the wheat;/ the dark house, the smoke, the bicycles, the airplanes/ that pass like thunder: and the children watch them;/ . . . I weep for a world that has died./ But I who sing am not dead./ If we want to go forward, we must weep/ for the time that cannot come back again, we must say no/ to this reality that has shut us inside its prison."[32]

La nuova gioventù is the best text for verifying the psychological and cultural itinerary of Pier Paolo Pasolini. I am of the opinion, however, that at the center of the drama, and therefore of the creative act, there lies the progressively more constrictive awareness of a loss of oneness with the "other self," so intensely recognized and loved—that essential image of youth recreated and lived in his relationship with self and with others, as far as possible, up to the fatal onset (biological, first of all) of a breakdown in the narcissistic balance that represented the basis—security and power—of the poet's existence.

The last allegory

The discourse of *Scritti corsari* and *La nuova gioventù,* as well as the poet's constant inclination to participate in other forms of cultural impact on literature, are expressed in the film *Salò o le 120 giornate di Sodoma* [Salò or the 120 days of Sodom]. As he had done in *Il Vangelo secondo Matteo* (The Gospel according to St. Matthew], in *Salò* Pasolini sets out to interpret a preexisting text, transferring to the Italian Social Republic of 1944–45 the plot of *The 120 Days of Sodom,* written in a cell of the Bastille by Donatien Alphonse Françoise, Marquis de Sade.

In an essay entitled "Abiura dalla Trilogia della vita" [Abjuration of the *Trilogy of life*],[33] traveling as always the road of public confession, the poet had discussed the problem of "anthropological genocide" in increasingly precise detail, thus anticipating the necessity for *Salò:*

> I abjure the *Trilogia della vita,* although I am not sorry I made it. In fact, I cannot deny the sincerity and the necessity that led me to the representation of bodies and their culminating symbol, sex. Such sincerity and necessity have several historical and ideological justifications. . . . In the first phase of the cutural and anthropological crisis that started toward the end of the Sixties—

when the unreality of the "mass-media" (and thus mass-communication) subculture was beginning to be triumphant—the last bastion of reality seemed to be the "innocent" bodies, with the archaic, dark, vital violence of their sexual organs. . . . Now everything is upside down. . . . Even the "reality" of innocent bodies has been violated, manipulated, tampered with by the power of consumerism: In fact, that violence against the body has become the most macroscopic datum of the new era for humans. . . . Where does the abjuration of the *Trilogia* lead me? It leads me to adaptation. . . . I am adapting to degradation and I am accepting the unacceptable. I am maneuvering to reorganize my life. . . . The present is before me, and alternatives are gradually fading away. I am revising my concerns for greater readability (*Salò?*).[34]

With the same vaguely maniacal logic of the negative rewriting of *La meglio gioventù,* Pasolini thus passes from the trilogy, which had proposed a fallen universe where sex was cherished as a moment of joyous, lively spontaneity, to *Salò,* a symbolic place where sex literally changes "sign." The result is in some way his moral testament, first because it is a somber allegory of Power (an entity the poet now conceives as metaphysical and metahistorical, and approaches with feelings of spiritual horror); and secondly because it uses "perverse sex," i.e., sadism, as a metaphor of the present field of action of Power, the true fascism of today. In the film, Salò's fascism is not, in fact, an object of historical analysis, but rather a narrative device.

The result is not a moralistic work (as a tracing of the landscape of hell could well be) because sexual authenticity ("sex as joy and pain," existential passion in its dialectic form) is given up for lost, and only the "suicidal delusion" remains. The hellish space of sexual perversity is privileged by Power—or rather, by the "anarchy of power," as the poet defines it—as a paradigm of the unconscious (or, in its historical and cultural aspect, of the irrational). The unconscious first emerges freely, then is diverted and distorted, with its "libidinous energy" institutionalized by that same power that would easily instrumentalize it in order to achieve its own ends. This is, I believe, the prophetic and obsessive vision of Pasolini.

It is obvious that the more or less obligatory choice of hyper- or bisexual symbols leads, in a movie, to the appearance of drastically repulsive images and sequences. These are barely redeemed (for a critical sensibility that stoically manages to witness the passage through the various Circles: the Circle of Manias, the Circle of Excrement, the Circle of Blood) and tempered by the decidedly anti-naturalistic style now favored by the director, and by the naive recitation of the damned, who are victims and executioners at the same time.

The ending of the film is unexpected and unique: Two young men, executioner-victims, dance awkwardly (one might even be tempted to say "innocently"), to the sound of the same easy little tune that punctuates—always at the critical moments—the sound track. They are speaking of the fiancée of one of them: "Yes, And her name is Margaret." With this name, this elemental allusion that inexorably recalls the final verses of *Faust,*[35] the film ends. This improbable opening to deliverance that seals the crowning moment of his violent refusal is the consequence of the choice Pasolini set for himself—with apparent difficulty and at least conflicting results—in the last of his "Corsair" writings and the last poems of *La nuova gioventù,* as a deliberate, "voluntary" act of faith in the future of mankind.

Pier Paolo Pasolini was murdered, or, more precisely, slaughtered, on November 2, 1975. Seven days later, the Italian government censor prohibited the showing of *Salò or the 120 days of Sodom* because "it brings to the screen images of sexual perversion so aberrant and repugnant that they are sure to be an offense against morals."

As a mortifying consequence, the first public presentation of Pasolini's last film took place not in Italy, but in France, at the Paris Festival. Censorship was later lifted, then reapplied, then lifted again. Beyond the intrinsic merits of the film, which are of course debatable, given its metaphorical violence and the general difficulty of interpretation, the legal briefs and the substance of the controversies surrounding *Salò* once again involved the author and the ideas expressed in his works, this time even beyond death.

Chapter Three
Posthumous Works

Il padre selvaggio

The year of Pasolini's death, 1975, was not only a time of intense, diversified intellectual activity; it was also the year in which the author revised and prepared for publication several works of various intent begun in different periods.

Il padre selvaggio [The savage father] had appeared in its original form in 1962 in *Film selezione* as the script of a film that was never produced. The final version of this work, not quite a short novel and not quite a scenario, elaborates the theme of the conflict between "history" and "prehistory," which had previously appeared as a central motif in several of the pieces in *La religione del mio tempo* (also written during the early sixties) and *Poesia in forma di rosa,* and was later developed in *Il Vangelo secondo Matteo.* In *Il padre selvaggio* "history" and "prehistory" are symbolized respectively by a young European teacher, a progressive lay missionary, and by the African adolescent Davidson Ngibuini. The transformation taking place in an African country which has recently won its independence (the reference to Lumumba's Congo [now Zaire] is explicit) frames the changeless, subliminal conditioning of the ancestral religion and the tribal rites, not excluding cannibalism. This is the setting for the story of a boy torn between allegiance to prehistory and submission to civilization, who comes, through his difficult contact with the white teacher, to find and then accept—not without trauma—his "identity" in history.

As often happens in Pasolini's works, different motifs and narrative structures are superimposed, leading to different and not always consistent interpretations. In a 1962 "conversation" edited by Nino Ferrero, the poet introduced the plot of the film he intended to make and underlined one of the fundamental themes:

It is the story of a poet. . . . Davidson, this is the name of the boy, writes beautiful themes, very poetic; but he is the most hostile to the teacher, the most tightly bound to the conventionalism he had learned from the colonialist teachers. At a certain point this boy goes on vacation, and during the vacation a situation like the one in the Congo explodes in his village. As a result, in this village where his father is chieftain, the boy undergoes a prehistoric, archaic experience of the life of savages, namely cannibalism . . . and he returns traumatized and neurotic. Gradually he frees himself from this neurosis by writing authentically liberating poems.[1]

It is not difficult to read the life of the poet Pasolini into the story of Davidson. If there were any need for confirmation, it could be found in the poem "E l'Africa?" [And Africa?], written in 1963 and emblematically placed by the author at the end of the book. Here the "savage father" at times assumes, through the conscious infringement on the coordinates of time and space that is one of the poet-director's stylistic devices, the concrete lineaments of Pasolini's own father: "*now it was only my father's face,/ with the gray skin of the drunk and the dying man,/* . . . Oh, father no longer mine, father and nothing but father,/ who comes and goes in dreams,/ when you will,/ . . . showing yourself to say terrible things,/ *to reestablish old truths,/* . . ."[2]

With the assiduous commitment to self-analysis that constitutes one of the pivotal points of his psychology, Pasolini goes beyond the merely emotional and identifies the conflict, painful and incurable, from which his poetry is born.

The 1975 version of *Il padre selvaggio* is a brief, exquisite work. The character of Davidson has a poetic substance that reveals the fondness for the subject and the maturity of the author. In the white teacher and his impassioned lessons on freedom and democracy we find, furthermore, the irrepressible pedagogic vocation which is expressed once again, in the last years of the poet's life, in the dialogues with Gennariello, an imaginary Neapolitan boy, first published in the weekly *Il Mondo* and later included, as prearranged by the author, in the volume *Lettere luterane* [Lutheran letters].

La Divina Mimesis

The publication date of *La Divina Mimesis* [The Divine Mimesis] is November 22, 1975, but the original inspiration of this short book goes back to 1963. In the poem entitled "Progetto di opere future" [Plan of future works] included in the collection *Poesia in forma di rosa,* the author in fact anticipates the title and the figurative forms of the work to come: "where into archaic, emphatic Hell/ . . . is inserted an insertion of the Hell of the neo-/ capitalist age, for new types/ of sins . . . to be integrated with the ancient ones."[3]

The stylistic function of the title—*La Divina Mimesis*—and the meaning of Pasolini's stylistic operation are clarified in theoretical terms in the essay "La volontà di Dante a essere poeta" [Dante's will to be a poet], written in 1965, when the problem of the relationship between linguistic instrument and literature was one of the author's main speculative preoccupations. In that essay he asserted that in the *Divine Comedy* there is a significant "immersion and total 'mimesis' by Dante in the psychology and social habits of his characters. And therefore a contamination of his language with theirs."[4]

In the second of the "notes" added by the poet to the first two cantos of his Inferno (the only ones published in completed form) we learn that as a mimetic recording analogous to Dante's, the infernal canticle of *La Divina Mimesis* was to be written in an "Italian that preserves, living and aligned in a real contemporaneity, all the diachronic stratifications of its history."[5] In the same note the author specifies further that, as a consequence, "all the prospects of the future—namely, the planning and construction (in progress) of the Two Paradises—neocapitalist and Communist—will be drawn up in the so-called new language: with its progressive sequences, . . . its absolute supremacy of communication over expressiveness, etc."[6] It is evident that Pasolini is here rekindling the substance of the argument against the corrupting influence of neocapitalism in a tone of gloomy irony, in the light of the conclusions reached in the famous 1964 essay *Nuove questioni linguistiche.*

The result of this outlined comedy of the contemporary "spirit" (of which Pasolini may have left other parts unpublished) is a work in which we find the sketchy prefiguration both of the apex of Pasolini's view of man—its final expression is *Salò*—and of the inescapable destiny of the author.

Pasolini, at the same time Dante and Virgil (the timid guide who symbolizes the contradictory encounter of passion with ideology), wanders in the midst of a damned humanity sunk in a bourgeois inferno. Every Circle and every Pit in it corresponds to a way of life as false as it is inescapable: the anonymity of the masses; enforced "normality"; the consumer ethic; conformity. The two "cantos" in prose are followed by programmatic announcements introducing an even more explicitly infernal "Paradise," as well as illustrative notes and remarks. At the end of the book a "faded iconography" acts as counterpoint to the "fragments of Hell": Included are the luminous images (one thinks of the symbolic function of light in Dante's "dark forest") of the "old truths"—post-Resistance Italy with its Communist Assemblies and the tomb of Gramsci—and images showing the stages of the irreversible process of totalitarian cultural homologization. The last image is that of the "African landscape" which, in the despairing vision of 1975, has also become a part of the "faded iconography," hopelessly relegated to the past.

As we have already observed with *Il padre selvaggio,* the posthumous pages of *La Divina Mimesis* also reveal—in this case through the controlled mixing of the various stylistic registers—a striking maturity. Objectively speaking, the work is incomplete; however, it possesses a structural solidity that guarantees its full autonomy.

Lettere luterane

The group of works whose publication had been prearranged by the author before his unexpected death includes *Lettere luterane* [Lutheran letters], published on November 27, 1976. This volume, a continuation of *Scritti corsari,* is a collection of the articles and especially the "interventions" published by Pasolini in 1975, up to the month of October, in various Italian dailies and weeklies. The "Lutheran letters" show the same civil concern that characterized the pieces of the *Scritti corsari* and manifest the same stylistic aggressiveness.

The title was expressly chosen by the author and, like that of *Scritti corsari,* suggests a self-definition which, in light of its contents, imposes more than a mere lexical or semantic interpretation. "Luterano," Lutheran, is a synonym of "Protestant" in Italian; and in this case "protestant" stresses the first meaning of the adjective, deriving from "protest" as active dissent in the midst of the guilty conformity of the Catholic-universal silence.

In the imaginary dialogues with Gennariello (more a disciple than an interlocutor) Pasolini continues the critical probing of the ethical, political, and cultural institutions through which the crisis of bourgeois society and its superstructures is revealed. Forced to record once and for all the no longer reversible change of the "absolute" reality in which he had come to place his hopes for salvation (the agrarian civilization of Friuli, the urban sub-proletariat, the no-longer uncontaminated Third World), the poet has by now assumed the limiting guise of the "polemicist," the dissenting intellectual whose mission (not always successful) is to appeal at all costs to the civil conscience of the Italians.

San Paolo

Pasolini had not arranged for the publication of *San Paolo* [Saint Paul] (1977), the project of a film on which he had begun work in 1968 and taken up again in 1974 without being able to complete it. In the book, the first draft (by the author emblematically dated May 22–28, 1968[7]) is followed by a sketch for a scenario developed in 1974 and an editorial note clarifying, at least in part, the theme of the text, which was evidently close to Pasolini's heart. We learn from the note that the author had intended to publish the sketches, after reworking them into a final form.

The transposition of Paul's existential situation into our time was to have been the basic motif of the film. Thus Jerusalem, "the ancient capital of power," was changed in the first version to Paris at the time of World War II and the Nazi occupation. In the 1974 version, New York, Rome, and London are a few of the many stopping-places in Paul's journeys for preaching and action in his contemporary guise. Through a further series of connected transformations, the background characters—Roman oppressors, persecuted Christians, Pharisees—become Nazi soldiers, partisans, and representatives of the conservative, reactionary bourgeoisie. The textual changes made in 1974 indicate an attempt to clarify what was to have been the central, highly problematic significance of the figure of Paul, ex-bourgeois collaborator during the German occupation, later a member of the Resistance, struggling first against the Nazis, then against the general conformism of our time. The function of the apostle, mystically converted to a subversive cause, is progressively and inexorably overshadowed by that of Paul the "organizer" and establisher of his own inflexible orthodoxy, founder of a dogmatic, powerful Church, "not a saint, but a priest." When the priest becomes a saint again, his message is no longer understood. The young and the intellectuals are first his allies and then his executioners.

The analogy with the polemic Pasolini waged against the leaders of the P.C.I. and the connection with the poet's fiery reaction to the student rebellion of 1968 constitute the primary interest of *San Paolo*. The unresolved complexity of the story and its protagonist is a direct reflection of the underlying tangle of ideological reference points. The work is the outline of a vision (probably supported by Pasolini's reading, between 1965 and 1968, of the works of Marcuse and other philosophers of the Frankfurt School) of a future of inevitable internal conflict within the bourgeoisie, destined to lead to anything but a revolution.

The evolution of the apostle, the mystic bearer of the Christian Word, into the "organizer" of the Church should be associated with the meaning of the verbal infinitive "organizzar" in the title of the collection *Trasumanar e organizzar*, the key poems of which were written around 1968, and with the specific poem "Trasumanar e organizzar" discussed above and the meaning of its polemic against the P.C.I. We should think finally of *Calderón* (published in 1973, but started earlier, in 1965) and the ambiguous character of Basilio, "not a Fascist but worse than a Fascist," yet the lucid bearer of Pasolini's fulminating analysis of the '68 pseudo-revolution as the regeneration of the bourgeoisie.

On the other hand, and despite the 1974 attempt to deepen it, the character of Paul seems to be drawn with little exegetical zeal. We find no evidence of the rigorous elaboration of biblical texts which had preceded *Il Vangelo secondo Matteo* and mark that movie. Passages of discourses taken from the saint's "Epistles" are linked, synthesized, or juxtaposed without any recourse to the hermeneutic instruments certainly not unknown to Pasolini.

The interest in the structure and potential of a work "with all rules suspended" already expressed in *Il Manifesto per un nuovo teatro* (1968) may have influenced the writing of *San Paolo,* as the continuous and explicit solicitations to the reader-audience through provocative questions and answers would suggest.

Pasolini was evidently aware of both the speculative boldness and the substantial open contradictions that bring about the structural weakness of this work, conceived during the period of outward poetic and narrative silence between the publication of *Poesia in forma di rosa* (1964) and *Trasumanar e organizzar* (1971). It was perhaps for that reason that he put off its revision and publication. *San Paolo* remains nonetheless a fundamental attestation to the depth of a crisis that gave rise to that desperate, lucid discourse on the future of capitalism, on its emptiness of values and the indisputable mechanisms of Power, that would accompany Pier Paolo Pasolini to the experience of *Salò* and to his death.

I Turcs tal Friúl

Written as a theatrical work in 1944 when the author was twenty-two years old, *I Turcs tal Friúl* [The Turks in the Friuli] was published in 1976, by the review of Friulian studies *Forum Julii.* Based on an event of past history—the third invasion of the Friuli by the Turks in 1499—the short play, written in dialect and set in Casarsa, is no less than significant.

On the one hand, it is easy to see the analogy between the situation of that time—the dismay of the peasants in the face of imminent invasion and the slaughter that would inevitably follow, with all the weight of uncertainty and death—and the factual circumstances of 1944, characterized by the Nazi occupation and the partisan war. On the other hand, for one who remembers the author's personal life and his position within the historical contingencies of his time—or rather outside them—the play takes up profound resonances, even in the utter simplicity of its structure and the fragility of its thematic development.

The two principal characters of *I Turcs tal Friúl* are brothers: The elder, Pauli Colús, remains inclined to moral discourse and existential reflections, while the younger, Meni, places himself at the head of a group of peasants and dies fighting against the Turkish invaders. The autobiographical correspondence—Pier Paolo's abstention from active intervention, the death of Guido in combat—might seem obvious if a careful reading did not reveal an unexpected awareness of the necessity of their choices. In his recent biography of Pasolini, Enzo Siciliano writes: "The contrast between the two brothers was a real one. The passion for freedom, the rejection of Nazism and Fascism on the part of Pier Paolo was not translated into action—or at least, it was translated into other action than that of armed struggle." In her comment on the 1976 edition of *I Turcs tal Friúl,* Andreina Ciceri further elucidates the function of the two characters: ". . . the two brothers Meni and Pauli (continually suggestive of the real brothers) do not seem to be two dichotomous presences, but—as if by chiasmus—two interchangeable souls. . . ."[9]

The identification with Guido beyond life and death, the acquired ability to objectify reality and the consequent passage from moral to political reaction constitute the deepest motifs of this youthful work. More readily observable are some of the themes that will become "archetypal" in the corpus of Pasolini's works: the presence of the uncorrupted peasant world, the vitality of the characters, and the menace, the incumbency of death as the incomprehensible and inescapable negation of life and youth:

> Today it is death that waits around us. Is it possible that all this must end? O Lord, what miracle is this, that you have to live again, when every thing around here that is now alive, as if it would stay alive for ever, will be destroyed, vanished, forgotten? . . . The smell of hay and wet grass, the smell of hearth-fires, the smells that we have known since boyhood, returning from the field.[10]

Thus in *I Turcs tal Friúl* we see the first critical awareness of phenomena about to be defined in their historical connotation, along with the presence of both the Friuli and Casarsa as constant reference points of the poet's universe.

Chapter Four
La meglio gioventù
The best youth

La meglio gioventù [The best youth] is the volume, published in 1954, that brings together the entire first cycle of Friulian poems: most of the *Poesie a Casarsa* (1941–48); the *Suite furlana* (1944–49); a group of poems directly linked to the events of the Resistance entitled *Il Testament Coran* (1947–52); *Appendice* (1950–53); and *Romancero* (1953). The latter group includes, under the subtitle *I Colús*—the surname of the poet's mother's family—the "humble" story of the Friulian land.[1]

The presentation in a single volume of a number of poetic works, written during different periods even if thematically and linguistically tied, seems to indicate the author's desire to clarify *a posteriori* the psychological and cultural structure of his first literary attempts. The fundamental choice is that of the Friuli as "the early characterization of an essential rapport, of a bond with a geographical, social, and even biological matrix"[2] conditioning the poet's whole discourse, up to the necessary ideal conclusion. Underlying the choice of the Friuli is the dialectal option shared by all the compositions of *La meglio gioventù* and constituting their most evident stylistic note. Speaking of himself in the third person, Pasolini has outlined the motives of the choice that made him assume the Friulian dialect as "his only mode of consciousness." In the essay "La poesia dialettale del Novecento" [Dialect poetry of the twentieth century, 1952], in the section on "Il Friuli" we read that

> at the sources of his sensuality there was an impediment to a form of direct knowledge from the inside out, from the bottom up . . . ; a screen had fallen between him and the world for which he felt such a violent, childlike curiosity. Being unable to possess it by the psychologically normal means of the rational, he could only re-immerse himself in it . . . return along that

road, at that one point when his moment of happiness coincided with the enchanting landscape of Casarsa, with a rustic life made epic by a heartrending charge of nostalgia. Knowing was the same as expressing. And here is the linguistic break, the return to a language closer to the world.[3]

The rejection of the official Italian language of the twentieth century thus imposes the retreat to a dialect which, for lack of other instruments of expression, becomes the chosen language. Regarding this option, it would be restrictive to neglect its political significance, albeit differently "political" with respect to the poet's whole later message, preceding as it does "the discovery of Marx." As I have already indicated, through his adoption of dialect in the early poems, Pasolini exalted, with true anti-conformism, that which the Fascist regime intended not so much to oppress as to exclude, namely the regional idiosyncrasies, the vital originality of local cultures, and the innocent naturalness of the peasant world. Opting for a world left outside the institutions, the poet carried on his literary operation against the nationalistic centralism of Rome and against the pseudo-intellectualism descending from it.

Beyond the courage and purpose of a political statement, and in a certain sense in contradiction to them, the recourse to dialect implies a rather complex process of poetic stylization. In the first poems, namely those collected in the short volume published in Bologna in 1942 under the title *Poesia a Casarsa,* the linguistic medium is "a literary koiné" utilizing words and expressions from the dialect of Casarsa and its neighboring villages (those on the right side of the Tagliamento River). The young poet had sensed the creative autonomy and the integral vigor of that vernacular, still relegated to the status of a spoken language, which made it unique even within the sphere of the limited but tested Friulian linguistic and literary tradition. With the philological acumen that would always mark him, and through survey operations showing a technique based on the codified rules of university linguistics, Pasolini gathered the living language, emitted "from the mouths of native speakers." The attestation is once again his own:

On a summer morning in 1941 I was on the wooden balcony outside my mother's house. . . . on that balcony, I was either drawing . . . or I was writing verses. When there resounded the word *rosada* [dew]. It was Livio, a neighbor boy from across the street, one of the Socolaris, who spoke. A tall, large-boned boy. . . . Anyway Livio surely spoke of simple, innocent things. The word *rosada,* spoken on that sunny morning, was only an expressive bit of his oral vivacity. Certainly that word . . . *had never been written.* It had always only been a *sound.* Whatever I had been doing that morning . . . I stopped suddenly: this is part of the dazzling memory. And I immediately wrote some verses in that Friulian speech . . . which up to that point had been *only a bunch of sounds:* I began at first to make the word *rosada* graphic. That first experimental poem disappeared; the second, which I wrote the next day, remains: Sera imbarlumida, tal fossàl/ a cres l'aga . . ." [Luminous evening, in the ditch/ the water grows.][4]

However reliable the "dazzling memory" might be, what undoubtedly struck the poet, activating his imagination, was the expressiveness of the intimate spoken language and its phonic substance; and he benefited, as Giorgio Caproni has written, from "the fact of having assumed a language . . . not properly his own, which not only did not force him, precisely because it was not his own, to choose and love its particular physical and human territory with a redoubled 'spirit of love'; but, being almost virgin as far as literature is concerned, also permitted him a greater freedom of speech thanks to the newness of the words, which were not yet codified and therefore still malleable."[5]

As we learn in a "note" by the author in the 1954 edition, the compositions in Friulian that follow *Poesie a Casarsa* show some changes with respect to the first group ". . . while there the linguistic 'violence' tended to make of the Casarsan speech both a Friulian koiné and a sort of absolute language, nonexistent in nature . . . here Casarsan is readapted in its entire institutional quality."[6] Several of the poems of the second group, furthermore, are based on other variants of the Friulian dialect: that of Valvasone, Cordenons, Gleris, etc.: all villages situated in the heart of the Friuli, on the right bank of the Tagliamento. The poet's philological attention to local variations is painstaking, and it is carried out through tonal differences pervading the various compositions and also in the use of similar—but not identical—words identifying or qualifying a single object, and in the multiformity of syntactical devices.

In my opinion, however, it is in *Poesie a Casarsa* that "the greater freedom of speech" permitted by words "not yet codified" is manifested more clearly, in the extraordinary richness of expressive variation afforded by the "speakers' " vocabulary and that of the poet.

To aid the average Italian reader and—given the special composite nature of the dialect in the early works—the Friulian reader as well, Pasolini has provided, at the bottom of the page, an Italian version of the various compositions, stating in the note to the 1954 edition "the versions in Italian . . . are a part, and sometimes an integral part, of the poetic texts: I have therefore drafted them with care and almost, ideally, at the same time as the Friulian versions."[7] With Pasolini, and contrary to the opinion of those critics who pointed out only the inevitable lack of "musical resonance" in the translations and the fact that they are only approximative interpretations (which, no doubt, is quite evident at times), I retain that they fulfill a notable structural function both within the individual compositions and in the collection as a whole. Within the full range of his Friulian works, the dialect text conveys the poet's yearning—originally lyrical—for a recovery of moral health to be acquired only through an immersion in the innocent naturalness of the peasant's world, the remoteness of which the poet feels with unconquerable melancholy. Detached from reality, taken on as a distant, absolute tongue, the dialect lives in its ability to evoke, evoking essence rather than existence. To the translation is given the task of "naming" in a recognizable fashion. In the pages of the book, the physical space between the dialect text and the translation the reader must consult in order to understand (a space which at times takes up most of the page) creates a further distancing from the poet's world.

This opposition—or juxtaposition—of dialect and translation can also be expressed as a contrast between the poetic functions of sound and meaning. Consider what Pasolini said about his first perception of the aural essence of Friulian: The dialect provides the poetic sound and substance, but we must resort to the translation to demystify the expression and to find access to its meaning.

Identification with nature and with people, the boy and the mother, the enchantment of the countryside, the arcane fascinations of religiosity and solitary sex constitute the general topics of the first part of the collection. They are placed between the polar presences of innocence and death. In the second part, which deals with adulthood (and the division is purely psychological), the same themes reappear, revealing, however, new interests, not so much social as moral, favoring the motifs of poverty as daily struggle, of a first, still-latent, and unconscious rebellion by the peasants against the rich, of a thirst for liberty understood as freedom from oppression of the natural right to be young and to be happy. The theme of the Resistance is also placed within this by-now-limiting framework, between youth and death.

In the economy of both parts, if to differing extent and with differing functional usage of stylistic elements within the whole of the text, the image of infancy and youth in all their attributes is preeminent, and the expressive richness of dialect assists the poet.

The lexical variants connoting children, boys, and youths are quite numerous, and the tonal shadings they express are, more often than not, impossible to render in translation; but they may be felt in the poetic context of dialect. The range of these expressions is again enlarged through adjectival qualifications.

Nini is the word connoting childhood. There follow those that designate early adolescence and youth: *frut, donzel* (of almost classic poetic stature), *fí, fantàt, zòvin,* and the variations *frutín, fantassín, fantassút, frutút, zuvinín.* The range of these locutions is further widened by qualifying expressions: *frut di lus* ("child of light"), *zòvin lizèir* ("light youth"), *bel fí* ("handsome lad"), *puòr zòvin* ("poor youngster"), *frut ch'al rit* ("laughing child"), *spirt di frut* ("boyish spirit"). (The more imaginative and affectionate of these variations are more numerous in the first part of the collection.)

The poem immediately following the "Dedica" [Dedication] to Casarsa introduces many if not all the allusive symbols of the collection, beginning with the title "Il nini muàrt" [The dead child] and the evocation of Narcissus. In the first tercet the landscape is luminously vital, marked by fertility expressed in nature and woman:

> Sera imbarlumida, tal fossàl
> a cres l'aga, na fèmina plena
> a ciamina pal ciamp . . .[8]

[Luminous evening, in the ditch the water grows, a woman with child walks through the field.]

Nevertheless, in the second part the picture dissolves and the luminous quality of the evening vanishes: "I remember you, Narcissus, you were the color of the evening, when the bells toll for the dead."[9] The evocation of memory, and especially the past "you were," interrupt the peaceful contemplation. There is an implicit relationship between the "I" and Narcissus: the "I" establishes the scene and the memory, then evokes and calls Narcissus. Narcissus is the device permitting the introduction of both the poetic voice and the symbolic premonition of death. In an atmosphere of subdued resonances, in which the "luminous" evening of the first tercet becomes the mere color of itself, the end is linked to the title. The symbolic poles of the work are revealed through the structure of the poem and the overlapping of images.

Narcissus

The first boy to emerge from the poet's memory in "Poesie a Casarsa" is called "Narcís," Narcissus. In other poems other boys and youths appear, and if their name is not Narcissus, they take Narcissus's lyric function. In *Poesie a Casarsa* and *Suite Furlana* (1944–49) especially, the name and presence of Narcissus return until they finally assume an unequivocal dimension:

O me donzel! Jo i nas
ta l'odòur che la ploja
a suspira tai pras
di erba viva . . . I nas
tal spieli de la roja . . .[10]

[O my youngling! I am born in the smell that the rain breathes from the meadows of living grass . . . I am born in the mirror of the fosse . . .]

And under the title "David":

"Leaning against the wall, poor lad, you turn towards me your kind head, with a weary laughter in your eyes . . ."[11]

up to the poem "Suite furlana" and the three variations of "Dansa di Narcís":

"A boy gazes at himself in the mirror, his eye laughs black . . ."[12]

. . . I arose among the violets
while the dawn was breaking
singing a forgotten song . . .
I said to myself: "Narcissus"
and a spirit with my face
obscured the grass
with the gleaming of his curls.[13]

The motifs connected to the myth of Narcissus are not, in my opinion, peripheral to Pasolini's poetic work, but they encompass all the other themes. By this I do not intend to claim that the myth constitutes the poetic archetype, but rather that the fundamental elements of the myth of Narcissus and those accessory to it are present in most of the poems of the first two groups. In the later ones, when the first glimmers of the social problematics surface, the myth is present on another level and takes on other colors, but it does not lose its function as a basic structure. Consider the last poem of *Romancero* (1953), cited above, the poem with the same title—"La miej zoventút"—that ends the book *La meglio gioventù:*

. . . Vegnèit, trenos puartaìt lontan la zoventút.[14]

[Come trains, take far away the youth.]

The poet's identification with the "merry youths" sent away from their land and condemned to laugh no more is obvious. Less evident is the link between the last poem in the collection and the first. If the Narcís of the first poem is a *nini muàrt, la miej zoventút* ("the best youth") of the last poem *va soto tera* ("goes under the earth"): This in fact is the following verse in an old Friulian folksong, from which the title is taken:

Sul ponte di Bassano
bandiera nera
la meglio gioventù
va soto tera[15]

[On the bridge of Bassano, banner of black, the best youth goes under the earth.]

The search for the elements of the myth of Narcissus in the compositions of *La meglio gioventù* reveals a singular balance between the energy and content of the poems and their formal characteristics. We find concrete presences: Narcissus and the other boys, the waters, the fountains, the tears, the mirrors, and—significantly in one of the last poems—*il flòur dal narcís* ("the narcissus flower").[16]

One component above the level of verbal imagery that governs the form of the work, connecting it with the substance of the myth, is the atmosphere of total stillness that in many compositions permits the reflection of the image:

I nas
tal spieli de la roja.
In chel spiele Ciasarsa
—coma i pras di rosada—
di timp antic a trima . . .[17]

[I am born in the mirror of the fosse. In that mirror Casarsa—like the meadows with dew—quivers with ancient time . . .]

The past within which the poet searches for himself is a reality retransmitted to us as a poetic image, and immobility is necessary so that the optical phenomenon of reflection may take place. Casarsa quivers "in the mirror of the fosse," but "like the meadows with dew" her stirring is placed within a poetic, figurative context that has the features of eternity. In the same way, "the woman with child" who yet "walks through the field" is immobilized as a characterizing pictorial element in the changeless scene in which Narcissus searches for and, in the dead child, recognizes himself.

Another stylistic structure that leads us back to the myth is the function of the echo. The Italian translation "echoes" the dialect text, and most of the poetry of the second drafting—*La nuova gioventù*—echoes that of the first version. Words and feelings become somewhat distorted, as words and sounds are when they are repeated by an echo. Thus the verse of the dedication "A no è aga pí fres-cia che tal mi país"[18] (There is no water fresher than in my village) becomes "A no è aga pí vecia che ta chel país"[19] (There is no water older than in that village). And the verses of the first form of "Aleluja": "Adès/ ti sos/ un frut di lus"[20] (Now you are a child of light) reecho: "Adès/ ti sos/ un frut mai vivút"[21] (Now you are a child who never lived).

If we continue reading *La meglio gioventù* examining the network of those metaphors that appear with high frequency, always in connection with the same ancient myth, we may glimpse the underlying affective forces and the decisive existential experiences that shaped them. We find the text invaluable in pointing out and exemplifying the author's persistence—up to the inevitable breaking point—in an attempt to realize (or simply to represent to himself) an ideal self, absolutely lovable for its truth, beauty, and power:

Io i soj un biel fí, . . .[22]

[I am a handsome lad, . . .]

. . . io i soj un spirt di amòur,
che al so paìs al torna di lontan.[23]

[. . . I am a spirit of love that to his place returns from afar.]

Lus a è me vita, e a súnin
di fiesta par me tal sèil nut, . . .[24]

[Light is my life, and they ring festively for me in the naked sky . . .]

The attempt to perpetuate a complete reproduction of himself and his own body is organized and concentrated around attributes or parts of his own physical concreteness. Of primary importance for the clarification of this aspect are the first two variations of "Suite furlana," which I transcribe only in part:

> Un frut al si vuarda tal spieli
> il so vuli al ghi rit neri.
> No content tal redròus al olma
> par jodi s'a è un cuàrp chè Forma . . .[25]

[A boy gazes at himself in the mirror, his eye laughs black. Not content, he looks in the other side to see if that Form is a body . . .]

The refusal to accept the reduction to subjectivity, marked by limitation and difference, is seen in the last of the *Poesie a Casarsa,* first version:

> A plòuf un fòuc
> scur tal me sen:
> no'l è soreli
> e no l'è lus.
> Dis dols e clars
> a svùalin via,
> io i soj di ciar,
> ciar di frutút . . .[26]

[A dark fire trains in my breast: it is not sun and it is not light. Sweet clear days fly away, I am of flesh, flesh of a child . . .]

To conclude this analysis, which well merits further study, there remains to be pointed out that determining element which, in the economy of narcissistic expansion and fixation as it appears in *La meglio gioventù,* is represented by the figure of the Mother. She comes to assume the role of an oracle of wisdom and authority that merges with her natural and immediate role as the object of desire, an image that is an obvious sign of a substantially regressive ideal ego, to the point where such an image may be recalled in the intact, absolute form of "Child mother" and "Girl mother." In "Pastorela di Narcís" the representation of the mother as the sensual image of a young shepherdess is set beside that of a fourteen-year-old Narcissus:

I olmi platàt . . .
e al so post i soj jo:
mi jot sintàt ta un soc
sot i ram dal pòul.
I vuj di mi mari
neris coma il fons dal stali,
il stomi lusínt
sot da l'abit risínt
e una man pojada sora il grin.[27]

[I spy hidden away . . . and in her place am I: I see myself seated on a stump, under the branches of the poplar. My mother's eyes, black as the bottom of the manger, shining body under the new dress, and one hand placed upon her lap.]

Exemplary of the mother's desire—desire by the mother—and furthermore of extraordinary poetic effect is "Suspir di me mari ta na rosa" [Sigh of my mother over a rose]:

Rosuta di me fí,
dulà ti àia ciolta,
parsè ti àia ciolta,
la man di me fí?[28]

[Little rose of my son, where did it pick you, why did it pick you, the hand of my son?]

Death, tenderly celebrated in *La meglio gioventù* (and in different ways in all of Pasolini's works where a relationship and identification with innocence and youth are expressed), is necessarily left outside the myth. The death of the archetypal Narcissus is not a real one, as the transition from the body to the flower is a resurrection, and the flower gives shape to the fundamental elements of transformation.

The meanings and the conclusive evidence of Pasolini's tormented narcissistic itinerary will be found in the pages of *La nuova gioventù*, all of them marked with the anguish of continual contradiction with reality. Mourning the elusive purity of virgin youth the poet will say there:

I no soj veciu jo
al è veciu il mond
che no muríntal lassa
cui ch'a vif sensa fond . . .[29]

[I am not old; it is the world that is old, which, undying, leaves those who live without a ground . . .]

And again:

i no plaus parsè che chel mond a no'l torna pí
ma i plaus parsè che il so tornà al è finít . . .[30]

[I do not weep because that world will not return, but I weep because its turning has ended.]

In the Friulian poems, essentially, Pasolini lives the paradox that the narrator—in Ovid's version of the myth—points out to the young Narcissus: "What you seek is nowhere; but turn yourself away, and the object of your love will be no more. That which you behold is but the shadow of a reflected form and has no substance of its own. With you it comes, with you it stays, and it will go with you—if you can go."[31]

Chapter Five
Ragazzi di vita
The marvelous and miserable city

More than twenty years after its publication *Ragazzi di vita* (1955) still is a paradigmatic work because it allows us to verify the genesis of Pier Paolo Pasolini's poetics and because of its place within the framework of the Italian literary scene of the time. If on the one hand *Ragazzi di vita* presents an indictment of a human reality captured in a state (which seems to be destined not to become a stage) of squalor and brutal misery, on the other hand we also perceive in it the temptation—all the more notable from the present viewpoint, in that Pasolini never entirely eliminated it—of finding in the social under-development of the Roman slums and in their condition of historical backwardness the surviving remnants of a primitive and substantially uncorrupted world.

The critical *querelle* following the publication of the book (beyond the immediate and heavily political reaction) places it within the debate over neo-realism understood as the affirmation of the inseparable relationship between involvement and expressive force, and as the link between the man of letters and the "new" reality following World War II and the Resistance. With the passage of time these attempts to interpret *Ragazzi di vita* according to a single determining literary current show a disturbing critical and methodological inconsistency, and seem motivated above all by the impulse to enter the general (though historically inevitable) debate over the meaning of culture and the function of the intellectual. However, some of the critical reviews also underline and elaborate the experimental bent which, in my view, by conditioning the style, becomes the verifiable identifying mark of the work and places it in a wider framework of discussion.

The rigorous sociological and ethnographic reconstruction of the sub-proletariat slum atmosphere underlying *Ragazzi di vita* dates back to Pasolini's first years in Rome and finds its first expression in the fragments gathered and published in *Alì dagli occhi azzurri* (1963). The distinctly experimental intention of this last book has already been pointed out.

Like many authors of his generation, and before most of them, Pasolini takes that body of ideas, of ethical, affective, and cognitive attitudes proper to the first half of this century reflected in "traditional" literature, and subjects it to a series (definitely not always consistent) of transformations, revisions, and adaptations. The inhabitants of the "marvelous and miserable city" are celebrated and redeemed in their daily "useless and irrelevant" bits of existence precisely because their very existence gives them an irrepressible dimension.

The fundamental difference between Pasolini's "sketches" (in *Alì dagli occhi azzurri* as well as *Ragazzi di vita* and *Una vita violenta*) and the *tranche de vie* of high naturalism is that the *tranche de vie* was intended to permit a more direct manifestation of the natural forces ruling human conduct. Pasolini considered the everyday, banal, even vulgar and obscene elements marking his characters and their world to be the most authentic, the ones through which existence is most directly expressed, because they have not yet been instrumentalized for the ends of prefabricated values.

The preview publication of the first and the fourth chapters of *Ragazzi di vita* in June, 1951, and October, 1953, issues, respectively, of *Paragone,* as well as the later changes, indicate the length and difficulty of the process of structural unification of the chapters and lead one to reflect on the partial autonomy shown by each of them in the final draft of the work. In the interview appearing in the *Fiera letteraria* of June 30, 1957, cited above (see chapter 2, n 1) Pasolini declared "The novel has the outskirts as its determining environment, and it requires a stylistic effort which is immediate, violent and mimetic."

The term *novel,* applied to *Ragazzi di vita,* had been fully debated and rejected in the final analysis by many critics, despite the fact that it appeared in the editorial note on the cover of the book. That the author himself stressed it—after two years, and necessarily with a critical awareness of the equivocation generated by that definition—

seems to indicate his programmatic intention. It is evident that the text is fragmentary. The book consists of eight long episodes which the author numbers as chapters, intending to underline their thematic unity and to indicate the pauses meant to mark the narrative rhythm, as well as the concluding necessity of the final chapter. Within the framework of this structure unfold the events involving the emblematic inhabitants of the marginal city between the last days of the German occupation of Rome and the early 1950s.

Against the backdrop of an urban landscape as violent as those who inhabit it, Riccetto and the others, in groups that come together and dissolve on the basis not of solidarity, but rather of the most immediate necessity, drag out their days and consume their unknowing existence. Their relations are never relaxed or trusting, and their individual and collective actions respond only to the impulse of instincts that are always sharp and never satisfied, like hunger and sex.

Ragazzi di vita lacks a central story or discernible linear plot, and if Riccetto appears more often than the others, his function is not that of protagonist. His story is rather the pretext for the introduction of the other stories and characters, fatally like himself.

On the other hand, there exists among the eight fragments a unity of a temporal nature allowing us to follow the precise flow of chronological time. This unity the author achieves through devices proper to the writing of the novel, such as the flashbacks—by which the various episodes are connected, if loosely—and the direct explanatory intrusions of the author or the comments of the characters. We may further note a programmatic coherence through which every episode is presented as an accidental variation on the recurring theme of the entire book: the frantic acquisition of "dough" and the inevitable loss of same. In the name of "dough" the temporary, occasional alliances of the co-protagonists form and break up, and their conscienceless cynicism and mocking, amoral shrewdness are manifested in acts and actions that become disconsolately conventional. They are not spared individual and collective tragedies and misfortunes, whose structural connotation is the apparent lack of motivation, but with very few exceptions, these fail to touch or change them.

The final chapter is manifestly conclusive, beginning with the title "La comare secca" [literally "The withered hag"]. In Roman parlance "the old hag" represents death. And death, at the filthiest point of the filthy river, takes away Genesio, who had, alone among the *Ragazzi,* shown in his extreme youth a pathetic generosity and the flickering of a conscience. The protagonists of the various episodes (who have been spared other deaths, much more casual and aridly unmotivated) are a chorus commenting on Genesio's disappearance. Riccetto himself, who had appeared in the first fragment incongruously dressed in a white shirt and gray trousers, is present—naked—at the drowning, and he backs away toward what will be, after all (in the ambivalence of Pasolini's ideology), his own death. Precariously inserted in the working world, which he understands and accepts only as a potential source of "dough" and consumer goods, Riccetto thus becomes the first—among Pasolini's characters—to make the fatal leap from an underworld that is pitiless and arrogant but substantially uncorrupted, into history and corrupting civilization.

Pasolini used Tolstoy's peremptory declaration as the introduction to the fourth chapter: "The people are a great savage in the bosom of society." The lyrical and thematic core of *Ragazzi di vita* is summed up in this statement. The people, in this case the sub-proletariat, appear trapped in a free and violent existence that allows neither development nor progress, condemned (or consecrated?) to remain outside society and history. Once again the myth of the people is identified, for the writer, with the myth of youth and adolescence and with the religion of "innocent sin." Such a religion presupposes and demands the intervention of death as its only guarantee of incorruptibility. In this sense the set of attributes of the "ragazzo di vita" is inevitably similar to that of the "little Friulian peasant" who preceded him in the fantasies of the poet and in the development of the man of letters.

The new language

It would be easy to connect the choice of the linguistic instrument devised by the author to express the world of the slum and its heroes with the use of dialect that had characterized the beginning of Pasolini's literary activity in what became *La meglio gioventù.* Since in the case of the novels one must speak of linguistic hybrids rather than dialect, it is likewise necessary to point out that Pasolini's recourse to Friulian dialect was, also, as I have stated above, the expression of an authentic process of poetic stylization, and that it therefore betokens a highly aristocratic intellectuality.

The linguistic mimesis of the Roman sub-proletariat achieved in *Ragazzi di vita* (and later, with quite similar results, in *Una vita violenta*) indicates rather an attempt to escape the literary language. In the face of a need to make his art an ideological instrument, Pasolini attempts to carry on an argument touching at the same time the ideal and cultural level and the level of language and style. Such an operation cannot be limited to the mimetic recording of a dialectal state, since the author must incorporate philological research into his own language, in order to transform that research into poetic imagery. The result is a composite narrative medium, drawn from the contemporary usage of diverse and contrasting linguistic modes and stylemes.[1]

Granted that textual verification on the basis of necessarily translated "samples" cannot be entirely satisfactory, I shall try to clarify, in outline, the substance of Pasolini's intent.

The contrast between vernacular, dynamic narrative and static descriptions is particularly evident in *Ragazzi di vita*. The vernacular, used almost as a chorus of the protagonists, rarely has the function of a dialogue, being rather interjective and exclamatory, characterized by an overabundance of jargon and trivial, frequently obscene, terms. Pasolini's attention to philological reconstruction both in the isolated remark and in the brief bits of real direct discourse is evident, and intended to preserve the expressive force of the local vernacular. To the same end the author uses the transcription of phonetic formulas that reproduce the pronunciation—quintessentially Roman—of initial geminates ("A pparagule!"—". . . te va bbè?"—". . . ieri a ssera").

The dynamic parts of the plot, constructed on the syntactic model of standard Italian, with greatly prevalent parataxis (at times underlined by the typical popular abuse of polysyndeta), are "contaminated" on the lexical level with dialecticisms and expressions drawn from the jargon of the young which, even more visibly in a narrative context than in the vernacular, take on the aspect of expressive points of a specialized language:

His brother was sleeping like a top, his mouth half-open and the sheets twisted around his legs. . . . Lenzetta, stoned out of his mind, went on singing with all the steam he had. Then his brother woke up with a start and said, "Hey!" "Fuck you," said Lenzetta, getting to his feet. His brother caught on to what was happening, looked at him, gave him a shove that slammed him against the wall, and dropped off again.[2]

The stylistic register used in the static descriptions is entirely different. The events are fully, sometimes elaborately, set in the natural environment in which they occur, and there are many reflective and lyrical passages. The syntax is always traditional, according to the standard language; however, it is rich in hypotactic constructions of a certain complexity, prevalently subordinates of various types. The punctuation is also traditional; commas graphically separate the elements of the sentences rather than marking off the rhythm of the images. The images, in their turn, are colorful, almost impressionistic; there are many cultivated, literary similes, and many repeated, refined metonyms:

It was a fine morning, the sun beating down on the Grattacieli, which looked clean and fresh, shining through miles and miles of blue and spilling a golden shower everywhere, on the gleaming humps of the Monte di Splendore or of the Casadio, on the façades of the buildings, on the inner courtyards, the sidewalks. And amid that golden freshness, people in their holiday clothes swarmed about in the center of Donna Olimpia, by the house doors, around the newspaper stands. . . .[3]
The moonlight bathed the entire plot, which was so large that the walls on the far side were out of sight. The moon was high in the sky by this time; it had shrunk in size and appeared not to want to have anything to do with the world, absorbed instead in contemplating what lay beyond. . . . At the end of the garden the light shone upon peach trees, willows, cherries and elders, springing up here and there in clumps as hard as wrought iron, twisted and insubstantial in the white dust.[4]

The images betray a note of decadentism, and the fact that they are set in a refined (and sometimes even precious) syntactic context contributes to accent the lack of tonal balance characterizing the various stylistic moods and, finally, the entire work.

In fact, on the vernacular level we notice the weight of experimental affectation, of the preponderance of the most unexpected forms of jargon—interesting philologically, but somewhat tiresome in their repeated application as attributes to the various characters. The result of this constant recourse to the popular word or phrase at the top of the voice, to the explosion of plebeian emotion, is the predictable uniformity of the characters and the fact that rather than creating, they appear to be created by their language. I have already stated, furthermore, that the intrusion of jargon finally remains extraneous and exterior to the dynamic narrative context, where it is, however, quite often present. Pasolini realized the need to accompany the two novels with brief glossaries, and this device seems to reaffirm the critical research which took place prior to the writing, and the author's concern that the language should be fixed within preestablished limits.

In the final analysis, there is no doubt that constant recourse to rhetorical and stylistic artifice weakens the entire structure of *Ragazzi di vita.* The gap between the author and his characters is made more apparent by the lack of integration among the stylistic levels of mimetic and philological operations, narrative captions, and reflective, lyrical moments. Notwithstanding the author's explanations and motivations, the contemporaneous use of different and contrasting linguistic models sets up a conflict between the objective and the subjective, and re-presents the opposition between a "matter" that must be expressed in its own terms and the individual comment of the artist.

By weighing these contrasts we can measure the limits of Pasolini's stylistic affirmation as well as the lasting significance of his ideology. If on the one hand we have the coldly analytic indictment of a reality captured in a state of brutal primitiveness, violence, and conflict, on the other hand we sense the critical presence of one who knows and cannot be silent.

As I have already mentioned, *Una vita violenta* (1959) takes the shape of Pasolini's reaction to the various imputations of the critics regarding *Ragazzi di vita.* Its novelistic structure is obvious: The "protagonist," Tommaso Puzzilli, shows (through an almost too openly schematized political iter) a "progressive" awakening, going from blind fascism to conscious acceptance of a socialist solution.

In this second Roman book the author corrects, furthermore, the excesses and the lack of balance of his linguistic experimentation in *Ragazzi di vita.* The syntactic organization responds to unitary expressive demands and, as a consequence, parataxis prevails both in the dialogue and in the explanatory and descriptive parts. The vernacular takes on the form and function of dialogue; jargon terms are assimilated into the descriptive passages, attenuating—if not entirely eliminating—the gap between the author and his characters.

Apart from certain qualitative differences of level between the various chapters—and sometimes between the sections of a single chapter—the dialect of *Una vita violenta* begins to lose the features of philological elaboration and becomes a genuine language, not so much recorded as lived and made real.

Chapter Six

The Ashes of Gramsci and Stylistic Freedom

Le Ceneri di Gramsci

One of the conclusions that may be reached in regard to *Ragazzi di vita* is that Pasolini was drawn to the "marvelous and miserable city" by "passion" and instinct rather than by rational ideological motivations. The poet intuitively realized how far he was from orthodox Marxism, and this awareness is lucidly analyzed both in the central poem of *Le Ceneri di Gramsci* [The ashes of Gramsci, 1957] and in the essay "La libertà stilistica" [Stylistic freedom]. The publication of the collection is placed chronologically between the publication of *Ragazzi di vita* and of *Una vita violenta,* and it is coincident with the drafting of the theoretical essay.

Le Ceneri di Gramsci is both an example and a further elaboration of the technical and thematic development—fundamental to the poet's message—hinted at in the last poems of the collection *L'Usignuolo della Chiesa cattolica* [The nightingale of the Catholic Church], published in 1958, but containing compositions written between 1948 and 1949. The poems "Paolo e Baruch," "L'Italia," and "La scoperta di Marx" [Paul and Baruch; Italy; and The discovery of Marx] are in fact dated 1948 and 1949, respectively: Following the "discovery" of Marx and beyond the lyrical idealization of the maternal universe of the Friulian peasant, they express, to varying extent and with varying poetic results, the moral dissent that imposes on Pasolini his interest in the "objective" living conditions of the lower classes, shut out from the national language and culture, suspended in their own metahistorical dimension.

This awakening of the poet's conscience is severely and painfully self-critical. It involves, in fact, a whole intellectual tradition, expressly bourgeois, forced to confront the contemporary moral and historical issues, within which the "ragazzi di vita" symbolize outward, objective reality.

All of the short poems of *Le Ceneri di Gramsci* are rigorously dated, but since their arrangement within the collection does not always correspond to their chronological order of composition, the poet seems to be stressing the need to approach the reading of the whole as a synchronic, circular unit. The study of the text in its rational and moral rhythm and the comparison of it with several theoretical essays written during the same period confirm this need. Analyzed one by one, the poems manifest the passage into the conscious, rationally motivated phase of Pasolini's instinctive populism; the poet's attempt to understand and internalize the ideology of the working classes; the resistance of the old Ego which—still circumscribed in its individual passion—clashes with the impulses of conscious ideology. The last poems, finally, record the drama of the events of 1956 and present the total reexamination of the poet's private world and the world surrounding and conditioning it.

In the first poems—"L'Appennino" [The Apennine, 1951] and "Il canto popolare" [The popular song, 1952–53]—written, as the author himself had declared, under the impact of his Roman experience,[1] the poet sets up a comparison between the Italy of yesterday and that of today, between a dark, yet splendid past from which the people are absent and a present that brings into the limelight a forgotten world in which there resides the only power capable of renewing history and canceling out injustice:

> An army encamped, waiting
> to make itself Christian in the Christian
> city, occupies a rotting stretch
> of filthy grass in the flaming countryside:
> he hopes to go down into the bourgeois
> light, awaiting a human
> habitation, he, the Sardinian or Pugliese,
> in a pigsty the muddy board
> in blind villages, between shining modern
> churches and skyscrapers. . . .[2]

The verses of "L'Appennino" are still openly emphatic; in "Il Canto popolare" we find preciously descriptive fragments that seem to be cut out of *Ragazzi di vita:*

> Boy of the people, you who sing,
> here at Rebibbia on the wretched bank
> of the Aniene, the new song, it is true
> that you boast, singing, the ancient, the festive
> lightness of the simple. But what
> hard certainty you also raise up
> of impending uprising, in the midst of ignorant
> hovels and skyscrapers, happy seed
> in the heart of the sad world of the people?[3]

"L'umile Italia" [Humble Italy, 1954] marks the passage from the vague humanitarianism of the first two poems to a more concretely defined populism, through an attempt to qualify and define Italian political reality:

> It is necessary to understand
> and to act: to believe oneself turned
> toward the best, overwhelmed by a sacrilegious
> daring to forget the dead,
> not to allow oneself a breath
> following the renewing of time.[4]

"Picasso," 1953, is the direct, if still strongly didactical forerunner of the central poem ("Le Ceneri di Gramsci") in that it identifies the task of the committed and involved artist in the midst of a divided and disintegrated society: That task is one of singing not the hopes of the future, but rather the reality and the despair of the present:

> In staying
> inside the hell with marble
> resolve to understand it; therein is salvation
> to be sought.[5]

"Comizio" [Assembly, 1954], critically introduces the theme of the Resistance as regressed and betrayed. (The same theme will be taken up again—from another point of view—in the central poem.) The image of the brother, emblematic of the "solarity" of the Resistance, is dialectically contrasted with the gray atmosphere of the "assembly," with its promise of pervasive officialism and heavy ideological stabilization:

> It is not the look
> of living people with me, this, in
> their faces there is a dead time that comes back
> unexpected, hateful, almost as if the good
> days of victory, the fresh days
> of the people, were themselves dead. . . .
>
> He asks for mercy, with that modest,
> forbidding glance of his, not for his own destiny,
> but for ours. . . . And is it he, too honest,
> too pure, who must go with lowered head?[6]

Pasolini wrote "Quadri friulani" (first appearing in *Officina* with the title "I campi del Friuli" [The fields of Friuli]) in 1955, on the occasion of an exhibit by the Friulian painter Giuseppe Zigaina. Despite its placement in the middle of the book and before "Le Ceneri," this short poem appears largely conclusive inasmuch as it stresses the contradiction—unresolvable for the poet—between a necessary rational concept of reality and the irreducible "irrationality" of life. Brought back to the idyllic world of the Friuli, Pasolini recognizes his own tendency to make up for himself a primordial cosmos, situated in a mythological time and disassociated from reality, and consecrated to an archaic refusal of history. Thus in the first part of the poem the mnemonic relationship is reestablished with the peasant universe, the extreme refuge of those who would save and guarantee themselves the uncorrupted image of an ancient innocence. The second part goes beyond both the merely emotive moment and the justification bound to the rhetorical and narcissistic taste of memory and proposes the fundamental issue of the central poem and of the entire collection. The poet recognizes in the works of his friend Zigaina a critical consciousness of phenomena, an ability and especially willingness to look closely at them and to define them in their historical connotation, which permits the interpretation of the Friulian universe as a society of "free men" who, finally removed from mythological time, are placed within the present and the future with their real conflicts.

"Le Ceneri di Gramsci" (1954) is in every sense the central composition which gathers up the complementary motifs of the poems which precede it in the arrangement of the collection and anticipates those of the following ones. Its historical and documentary importance, beyond the poetic, lies in its vivid rendering of the contradictions of the contemporary Italian scene and the collective conditions that derive from it, as reflected in the poet's consciousness. The entire poem is constructed around a scheme of the contrast between bourgeois background and Marxist commitment; between the ideal of freedom on the one hand and hypocrisy and political arrogance on the other; between a tenacious love of life in its most authentic and least rational manifestations, and the obligation to redeem this very life through political and class struggle, making a definitive choice. Antonio Gramsci becomes the model of that serious dimension of conscience and that clarity to which Pasolini, in the complex travail revealed in the various parts of the collection, aspires.

Before Gramsci's tomb,[7] on a dark May day, the poet sets forth the fundamental cruxes and the significance of his crisis, felt as an inability to find peace in the interpretations and the suggestions of an ideology. Despite the fact that he has accepted it with all his heart and "in the light" (that is, enlightened by reason), ideology is rejected by the ever-present irrational life:

> I subsist
> because I do not choose. I live in the non-willing
> of declining postwar: loving
> the world I hate—in its misery
> lost and disdaining—for an obscene scandal
> of conscience . . .
> The scandal of self-contradiction, of being
> with you and against you; with you in the heart,
> in the light, against you in the dark innards; . . .[8]

The character that emerges appears to us as much in need of moral authenticity as he is conscious of the irretrievable lack of a serious dimension of conscience, in the face of the progressive movement of reality.

In talking about *Le Ceneri di Gramsci* as a collection Franco Fortini has identified the synchysis as the most frequent and apparent rhetorical figure of Pasolini's contradiction.[9] If we examine the central poem in the light of this fundamental critical premise, it appears once again exemplary. Beginning with the title "The Ashes of Gramsci" where "there is the crude juxtaposition of the emotive, visceral term (the ashes) and the absolute rationality of the proper noun. . . . ,"[10] the poetic language is naturally arranged in oxymoron structure, and not only through the association of contradictory terms and adjectival and adverbial "corrections" (blind clearings; autumnal May; impurely healthful; ungodly piety; hard elegance; rough splendor; impure virtue; wonderful sewers, etc.), but also through continual antitheses of presences and images, and brusque juxtapositions of abstract and concrete. In the English cemetery—"wretched and noble garden"—Gramsci lies alone among other dead who are unlike him in every way, and still participates in their closed, abstract civilization:

> In the circles of the tombs the lay inscriptions
> on these gray stones, short and
> imposing, only show the lasting
> fate of lay people. Still by unchecked
> passions without scandal burn the bones
> of the wealthy of larger
> nations; there buzz, as never lost to view,
> the ironies of princes, of pederasts, . . .
> Here the silence of death is the faith
> of civil silence of men who have remained
> men. . . .[11]

The quiet cemetery is besieged by the bodily presence of the city that surrounds it, "indifferent." And it is the very "soil" of the city that "fat with nettles and pulses yields these slender cypresses."[12]

In "Le Ceneri di Gramsci" the contradictory richness of textual signs on the semantic level is correlated more visibly with the metric structures, which, because they are essentially common to all the poems, will be discussed at the end of this chapter.

At first reading, "Récit" (1956) seems detached from the progressive context of the collection, since it is clearly connected by the source of its content to the charge of obscenity that had been levelled against *Ragazzi di vita* and to the trauma caused the poet by that charge. The openly autobiographical tone and the substance of the poem clearly displeased Alberto Asor Rosa: "The motif of the man 'despised and rejected' becomes in 'Récit' an attempt at autobiography, childish protest, entirely without vigor. The charge of obscenity against *Ragazzi di vita* brings forth a tearful reaction in Pasolini, a questioning commiseration that asks for mercy, pity. The poet opposes the moralism of his accusors with his own moralism."[13]

To my way of thinking, however, the composition defines the development of the conflict, never to be resolved, between Pasolini and the institutions of power. The deeply personal antecedents and their juridical aspects in reality permit the externalization of the conflict between the direction of the author's poetics and the code of ideological values of the dominant culture. Indubitably, by weighing these conflicts we can measure the innovative aspects and also the serious limits of Pier Paolo Pasolini's literary ideology. In this poem the tension toward history and society remains in any case active and contradictory.

As for the function of "Récit" within the context and the structure of the collection, I subscribe to the position of Gian Carlo Ferretti: "It was said that 'Récit' seemed to carry us back several years; is it not rather the foreshadowing of a return to the original mythology, which will flourish again with greater strength than before, as soon as Pasolini has touched the bottom of his wounded conscience and his explanation of himself to the world?"[14]

The last three poems in the collection, "Il pianto della scavatrice" [The cry of the excavator], "Una polemica in versi" [A polemic in verse], and "Terra di lavoro" [Working land] are all dated 1956, and this clearly connects them to one another. Equally clearly, however, they are different in that they represent a development of one another. "Terra di lavoro," the last composition in *Le Ceneri di*

Gramsci, leads us back to the desolate vision of a sub-proletariat doomed (or consecrated?) to the same destiny of oppression and isolation that the first poems had brought to light and that history reaffirms, after having given cause for hope.

We should at this point remember what 1956 meant to Italy and to the rest of the world, especially the Communist countries. From February 14 through 26, the Twentieth Congress of the CPSU (Communist Party of the Soviet Union) was held in Moscow, during which Khrushchev presented the report attacking the person and the role of Stalin, revealing his crimes. When after several months the report—first kept secret—reached Italy, the repercussions were immediate. There were immediate statements of political and ideological position, going from specifically and violently anti-Stalinist polemic to the stated necessity of interpreting Stalin's actions in the context of history and determining the accountability of the regime.

What Pasolini had foreseen (he had always rejected the more peremptory ideological and normative formulations) appeared at this point to be confirmed in the new general need for a Marxist solution as anti-dogmatic as possible.

"Il pianto della scavatrice" is built around the symbolic motif of the excavator that inescapably transforms the free, wild archaic world, once again presented in its most deeply felt and loved aspects in the long excursus constituting the first part of the poem:

> [the excavator] Weeps for what
> ends and begins again. For what was
> grassy ground, open space, and is made into
> a courtyard, white as wax. . . .
>
> . . . and is made into a new block, swarming
> in an orderliness that is dull grief.
> It weeps for that which changes, even
> to become better. . . .[15]

In the complex structure of this longest poem in the collection hope is objectively perceived, never subjectively accepted:

See now, if you're alight
with hope—which, old lion
stinking of vodka, from his offended
Russia Krusciov swears to the world—
See how you know you're dreaming.
Each seems to burn in this happy August
of peace, each of your passions, each
of your inner torments
each naive shame
at not being—in sentiment
at the point where the world renews itself. . . .[16]

The critical conclusion—however conveniently schematic—of those who would see this first composition of the final triad as the song of hope, followed in the other two and especially in the last by the explosion of hope betrayed, seems too easy to me.

The sub-proletariat "enters" painfully and with difficulty into existence and into consciousness; the slum, "the marvelous and miserable city," yields to the world of work, but the poet still sees, unwilling and unable to deny it, the heartrending contradiction between the precise rationality of social and progressive opportunity and the fatal attraction of its "old snuggling of love." The workers, meanwhile, raise "their old red rag of hope." Contradiction, which remains even if the polar becomes the dialectical, still constitutes the historical-poetic structure of Pasolini's discourse.

"Una polemica in versi" reflects the moral climate of Autumn, 1956, and the dramatic consequences of the diffusion of Khrushchev's report: the political turnings in Poland and Hungary, and the bloody repression by the Soviet armed forces. In a note at the end of the book the poet reaffirms the polemic substance of the composition which, according to Gian Carlo Ferretti, takes as its target "bureaucratic crystallization, tactical devices, the 'diachrony' between political base and party, the leaders' inability to interpret the masses' 'hunger for history'. . . ."[17] The structure is that of a direct dialogue confrontation with an anonymous militant Communist, still strong but, like the poet, now "bitter" and "disillusioned:"

> . . . with what you have had
> for ten years inside, so clear
> that between the world and the mind it was almost idyllic . . .[18]

Now, the error must be recognized if the crisis is to be overcome:

> Your grief
> at no longer being in the front lines
> would be more pure, if at the time
> when the mistake, even if it's pure, is to be paid
> you had the strength to declare yourself guilty. . . .
>
> . . . you have accustomed yourselves,
> you slaves of justice, you ranks
> of hope, to the necessary acts
> that humiliate the heart and the conscience. . . .
>
> . . . Blinded by doing, you have served
> the people, not in their heart
> but in their banner. . . .[19]

In the generally sententious context of the poem we find again, enriched with a new and exemplary dimension, Pasolini's poetic mythology of the people. The "party," conceived as a hopelessly reductive intermediary, imposes the heavy presence of its apparatus at the celebration that should have belonged to the people, and the celebration gradually assumes an aspect of ambiguous sadness. There are the young people who live in hope, in their instinctive generosity:

> the supple youths
> in their festive clothes, rich
> with ribbons, kerchiefs, are nearly crazy
> with anticipated joy under Mexican
> hats, red as blood, and through clearings
> and clumps of trees they move in disorganized
> squads, in herds, alone,
> chewing American gum, in
> their shameless generosity.[20]

The adults and the old are instinctively aware of defeat:

> The men, already lost in an abject
> drunkenness hidden away like a sorrow,
> follow along behind their families gathered
> around the picnic basket. . . .[21]
>
> And look, uncertain, an old man lifts
> his cap from his white head,
> grasps in a new gust of passion
> a banner straight from the shoulders
> of someone in front of him, to his breast
> he presses it. . . .
>
> . . . Then the song, that had been raised
> joyous, desperate, ceases, and the old man
> lets fall the banner, and slowly,
> with tears in his eyes,
> pulls the cap down on his head.[22]

This "vignette" has collected somewhat mixed critical conclusions. In my opinion, Pasolini has given a courageous, solid dimension to the state of crisis that he, before anyone, had divined in its full meaning, and the poem assumes characteristics at once utopian and destructive, entirely original in the Italian literature of the 1950s.[23]

The last part of "Una polemica in versi" is clearly linked to the last poem in that it introduces the motif, central to "Terra di lavoro," of a humanity once again rejected by history. "Terra di lavoro," in its turn, brings us back to the first composition—"L'Appennino"—and to the formulation of an inescapably conditioned human destiny. On the train that "runs half empty" through the "land of work" (presumably the area south of Rome), the poet observes, with the compassion of one who has the wealth of knowledge and the privilege of thought, "the wan Southern passengers," restored to their atavistic hunger and to their fierce elemental existence, but without the "pure shadow of hope" that once was there:

> Their only law had ever been
> servile hatred and servile joy: yet
> in their eyes one could read
> at last a sign of a different hunger—dark
> as that for bread, and, like it,
> necessary. A pure
> shadow already taking the name
> of hope.[24]

Hopelessness constitutes the essential difference between "now" and "then," between "Terra di lavoro" and "L'Appennino," in which—in the words of Asor Rosa—we found "the conviction, ideologically quite explicit, that a presumed liberation of Man can be realized through an alliance . . . between a progressive, rational yearning and a popular thrust, fundamentally instinctive and irrational."[25]

The circular relationship of return and comparison between the two poems must be stressed. The vision of the "humble people," consistently present throughout the range of Pasolini's experience, now appears heavily conditioned by the radical change of political perspective before and after 1956.

The notion of a mythical immobility and a lack of historical awareness on the part of the sub-proletariat are evident in the last composition as in the first. In "L'Appennino," however, a dialectic relationship exists between the marble imperviousness of history (metaphorically represented in the recurring image of the "closed," "massive," "deep" eyelids of the famous statue of Ilaria del Carretto) and the thrust of the people to enter history, to "make themselves Christian," where "making oneself Christian" should be interpreted as a dynamic tension toward a redemption implying both rational and historical meanings.

In "Terra di lavoro" such a relationship is exhausted and the people can no longer be ascribed even to the dimension of myth. The images are ones of desperation: The little stream that cuts through the working land is "black as a drain"; "the autumn frost veils the sad wood"; "inside here is the sign of the dead"; the face of a youth is "small [and] dark as peat."

The prehistorical condition is expressed in a series, new in its significance, of animal similes: "miserable and dark as dogs"; "life of a lamb"; "like a beast that plays dead"; a flock/ of those who nothing else than misery know"; "by the faithless misery . . . of an abandoned dog."

The distance between the human reality of the southern passengers and that of the writer cannot be overcome. Not coincidentally, the poetic "I" speaks much less often here than in the other works.

After 1956, the "alliance" of which Asor Rosa spoke is no longer possible. The people are now completely "other," closed and hostile, an aggregate of monads who do not communicate: "This one, if you watch her, does not move"; "Then starting again to rock, blind, deaf"; "in a soundless smell of a sheepfold"; "[she] does not see the stranger/ [she] sees nothing." The poet, objectively a part of the very evil he subjectively suffers and condemns, cannot even offer compassion:

> You lose yourself in an inner paradise
> and even your pity is their enemy.[26]

The notion of experimentalism

In Italy *Le Ceneri di Gramsci* won the Premio Viareggio as an "experimental" work. It must be remembered that the value of this adjective is relative to the Italian cultural situation. In the August 16, 1957, issue of the *Times Literary Supplement,* in a thorough investigation of contemporary world literature, the section dedicated to Italy (XII) introduced the author of *Le Ceneri di Gramsci* as a representative of a "new" poetic tendency toward social significance. He was considered to be quite different from the other contemporary Italian poets in that he favored positive and rational forms, to the exclusion of the lyric.

In the essay "La libertà stilistica," published in *Officina* contemporaneously with the first edition of *Le Ceneri di Gramsci* in June, 1957, Pasolini gives us a precise key to the reading of the poems, showing their intention and experimental function. In and of itself the essay is very important because it clarifies the notion of experimentalism—in the context of historical dynamics—as the historical reason for literature. According to Pasolini, experimentalism is innovation of an intellectual and moral matrix, worked out within a commitment that does not necessarily coincide with a particular political choice.

The polemic target of the essay is the concept of "stylistic freedom" as it had been conceived in Italy during the early part of this century, irrational and exquisite but fundamentally illusory: ". . . in work of that sort one could not escape the intoxicating sense of being extremely free: almost as if there were no end to the chain of inventions. . . . But in that freedom there was neither choice nor suffering: and it could make one work in just one direction, toward the inside: and because of that the constraint of such freedom was rigorous."[27]

The allusion to the personal poetic experience of the author is manifest and, as always, profoundly honest. Laboriously and through complex paragraphs, Pasolini proposes the concept of "stylistic freedom" as parallel to poetic license. Such license necessarily costs dearly in that it forces an attitude that can appear undecided and problematical, but it is a sine qua non of any free-flowing poetic expression. Any "stylistic freedom" would be illusory, which is to say nonexistent, if it were fixed in the institutions of thematic and linguistic absoluteness, comfortably supported by certain official ideologies through which relational life is to be interpreted, and upheld by "closed" conceptions of the world like Catholicism or Marxism: once again without "choice" or "suffering."

The rejection of such an "illusory freedom" imposes active, open debate over the moral and historical problems of the time: "The same passion that with factious, naive violence had made us adopt the stylistic institutions imposed by free inventive experimentation, now leads us to adopt a moral problematics, in which the world that had been, at first, a pure wellspring of sensations expressed through a clever and exquisite irrationality, has now become the object of consciousness, ideological if not philosophical: and it imposes, therefore, stylistic experiments of a radically new kind. . . ."[28]

At the end of the essay Pasolini presents his own coherent literary proposal: ". . . it is clear that following the crisis, and the rejection of that full, enclosed world—going forward, to infinity, only on the inner front—the language that had been *brought up in its entirety to the level of poetry,* tends to be *brought down in its entirety to the level of prose,* or of the rational, the logical, the historical; with the implication of a stylistic effort exactly opposite to the one that went before."[29] Here is the introduction to the poetry of *Le Ceneri:* "experimental" in that it represents an attempt to give voice to a "moral problematics," to a conceptual, civilized effort, expressed "on the level of prose, or of the rational, the logical, the historical"—possibly an ordinary proposition in the context of other literary civilizations, but one rarely to be found in Italy. Whether or not Pasolini succeeded (as he wished) in withholding from his verses any openly lyrical meaning or intention is another question. We have already observed that in *Le Ceneri* one can often find a refinement and a bent toward decadentism all the more natural for being involuntary. They reveal the poet's inability to exclude them entirely—in literary practice—from his stylistic institutes, and to arrive at a thoroughgoing rationalization of his own intellectual search.

The reduction of poetic language

For Pasolini, the affirmation of stylistic freedom as innovation presupposes the pursuit of techniques that permit the reduction of poetry to prose and the consequent "lowering" of poetic language. In *Le Ceneri di Gramsci* this "reduction" may be noted on two levels. On the one hand, the poet moves away from the discounted poetic hierarchies. On the other hand, "reduction" is accomplished through the destruction of the verse and the stanza as both rhetorical and melodic units, in order to impart as prose-like a movement as possible to the rhythmic phrase.

The starting point, if not the immediate model of what for organizational necessity I have introduced as the first aspect of Pasolini's operation of stylistic reduction (without wishing to assert its preponderance over the second), is to be found in Pascoli, and more precisely, in his *Poemetti.* Here, more than in others of the numerous collections that make up the corpus of his works, Giovanni Pascoli created unexpected juxtapositions of images, from a poetic perspective that subverts empirical space, leveling objects and events and altering their relationships and proportions. To Edoardo Sanguineti we owe a lucid analysis of Pascoli's poetic operation, intended to clarify its ideological motives. These motives, taking into account their historical and personal differences, are analogous to Pasolini's "reasons" and to the need he felt and stated to reduce poetry to the language of prose. Sanguineti holds that: "the so-called poetic revolution waged by Pascoli is really a reformation, a profound reformation that develops as the transposition of a vast set of thematic and linguistic material from an area we may call, still schematically, haut-bourgeois, into a petit-bourgeois area."[30] And again: "Among the European irrationalists of the last century, if a very definite merit is to be ascribed to Pascoli, it is precisely this lowering: . . . the unequivocal clarity and total fidelity with which the open connection between social ideology and poetic perspective comes to be achieved in his work."[31]

Cesare Garboli is referring to Pasolini's analogous operation in *Le Ceneri di Gramsci* in the specific area of style, when he says that "Pasolini names a tram in the same way he names a plane tree."[32]

The second aspect of the "reduction" performed by the poet takes an extremely complex shape, "contaminated" as it is by his irrepressible—not to say irrational—tendency to destroy the rhythmic contexture of the verse in its components of syllable and stress, and the closed scheme of the strophe, by breaking the rhythmic concatenation.

All the poems of *Le Ceneri di Gramsci* can be analyzed in terms of traditional Italian prosody. Most of them are written in hendecasyllable tercets. The metric base of "Récit" is the double septenarius (line of seven syllables), otherwise defined as the "false Alexandrine" because of its resemblance to the classical French verse used in the romance on Alexander the Great. "Il Canto popolare" is in strophes of nine hendecasyllables, with frequent inclusions of lines with less than the full complement of eleven syllables. "L'Umile Italia" is also composed of nine-verse stanzas; however, its basic verse is the line of nine syllables, which may at times have one or more syllables in excess of the normal. Traditional Italian prosody dictates that the last stress fall on the penultimate syllable, or the syllable considered to be penultimate. In practice, after the last stress, one always counts one—and only one—syllable. The hendecasyllable—blank or combined in strophes of various types—is the most widely used of all Italian verses in all periods. Pasolini used it mainly in the historically consecrated combination of the *terzina dantesca* (terza rima), but deliberately subverted its traditional structure.

There is a recurring use of enjambment in a multitude of variations, on the level of both verse and strophe. Enjambment as a formal violation of the syntactic continuity and the sense of the statement involving the verse is too well accepted a rhythmic figure to require the presentation of examples, except in the cases that are technically least common. It is necessary to note, however, that Pasolini used it to an extent that goes far beyond tradition or the norm (however difficult these may be to establish). The consequence is a characterizing continuation of the rhythmic phrase, which no longer coincides with the single verse but is prolonged, forming a syntactic link between groups of successive verses, assimilating them to the patterns of discursive thought.

The forcing toward prose is accomplished by numerous technical devices which, in varying ways, slow down the reading of the rhythmic phrase and especially of the eleven-syllable line.

There are a great number of verses ending in words that are not semantically autonomous. Here only a continuous reading involving the following verse on the most basic level of syntax guarantees their meaning: (Given the schematic quality of the examples, I have decided to present them in the original Italian.)[33]

P.V. p. 127–masticando gomma americana, *nella*
(in the . . .)
C.G. p. 74–familiari da latitudine, *e*
(and . . .)
P.S. p. 108–del conoscerlo—*come*
(as . . .)

A high level of rhetorical attention is exhibited in the composition of hypermetrical hendecasyllables, lines to which one or more syllables—or even a polysyllabic word—are added. Such lines recur with notable frequency: The effect is on the one hand the dissolution of the traditional rhythm, and on the other hand the slowing of the reading. This slowing is even more evident when, in a very complex variation of the enjambment, the added word amplifies—but does not conclude—the meaning which the original structure would have left in suspense and which the following verse takes up and completes:

C.G. p. 75–E, da questo paese in cui non ebbe *posa*
la tua tensione,

And, from that land in which was without *pause*
Your tension

C.G. p. 76—nella sua miseria
sprezzante e perso—per un oscuro *scandalo*
della coscienza. . . .

—in its misery
disdainful and lost—by a dark scandal
of conscience. . . .

(The dash indicates a pause substituting for the eleventh syllable of the original line—before *scandalo* is added. Suspension points are in the original text.)

Quite often the verse requires either the last word of the preceding line, or the first one of the following line, to achieve the traditional rhythm:

P.S. p. 98–piazzali di mercati, tristi
strade
large market squares, sad
streets

At other times the opposite happens, as it is necessary to eliminate the first word of the line to reconstruct the hendecasyllable:

C.G. p. 75–*morti:* Le ceneri di Gramsci . . . Tra speranza

We find examples (the preceding is not one of them) in which the length—if not the rhythm—of the hendecasyllable can be reconstructed if one obeys the suspension points (or the dash, as in C.G., p. 76) indicating a pause, which take on the value of the missing syllable. Once again the sense of the discourse is preserved by a reading that overlooks prosodic constraints:

C.G. p. 107–pure della vita . . . si riduce

The variations in speed most often parallel the effects on rhythm. In any case, the examples I have cited up to now reveal Pasolini's sometimes obviously experimental interests and his decision to find in prose a fitting vehicle of poetic thought.

It is useful now to indicate several of the many strategies which, especially in the central poem and the last ones, subvert the metrical organization of the verse and the strophe. In order to understand the extent to which the rhythmic balance is upset, and notwithstanding the obvious fact that the judgment of the euphonic qualities of any poem is to a certain degree subjective, one must take into consideration a few basic facts about the Italian language in its poetic manifestations, that make it quite different from English. Due to a relatively limited number of word endings, Italian rhymes easily, thus Italian poetic tradition is less tolerant of rhyming licenses and of "imperfect" verbal correspondences.

The relative variety of the Italian hendecasyllable is assured by the fact that its rhythmic stresses are not fixed, except for the last, which falls—always—on the tenth syllable. The poet's will to transgress is doggedly concentrated on the tenth syllable of "his" hendecasyllable, but the intermediate stresses too are displaced in a practically infinite series of combinations.

The violation of prosodic structure on the level of the strophe actually strikes the eye of the reader. Having chosen terza rima as the basic meter for most of his poems, Pasolini proceeds to upset its rigorous rhyme scheme. Whole tercets are characterized as such only by typographical division; and in them it is practically impossible to reconstruct the hendecasyllable:

P.S. p. 116–quasi non avesse meta,
un urlo improvviso, umano,
nasce, e a tratti si ripete.

almost as if it had no goal
a cry, unexpected, human,
is born, and at times is repeated

Mixed in with the hendecasyllable and inserted in the tercet we find shorter verses with seven, eight, or nine syllables, preceded or followed, however, by a hypermetric hendecasyllable long enough to permit the reconstruction of two regular hendecasyllables:

> P.V. p. 123–batte dietro l'immoto miraggio del costume—
> gli inutili angoli sperduti
> del mondo, con qualche grido, qualche lume,
>
> [he] scans behind the motionless mirage of custom—
> the useless scattered corners
> of the world, with some cry, some light,

Distracting imperfect or near rhymes are only too frequent and they are sometimes echoed by internal rhymes and submerged alliteration. Assonance and consonance occur in their variations. "Light" rhymes (where the final rhyming syllable of a word is unstressed) are copious as are identical rhymes (achieved by repetition of the same word). (Examples intended to illustrate the expedients mentioned above would require an oral reading and a careful interpretation of the phonetic components.)

In traditional Italian usage of the terza rima, the conclusion of a larger formal unit is somewhat—but not necessarily—emphasized by a single line rhyming with the middle one of the preceding and last tercet, thus completing the rhyme pattern. The effect of linkage is eliminated by Pasolini:

> P.S. p. 118–che ci dà vita, nell'impeto gobettiano
> verso questi operai che muti innalzano
> nel rione dell'altro fronte umano,
> il loro rosso straccio di speranza.
>
> that gives us life, in Gobetti's like impulse
> towards these workers who silent raise
> in the tract of the other human front,
> their red rag of hope.

Although Pasolini's drive against metrical organization can be verified in all the poems of *Le Ceneri di Gramsci,* the distribution of the strategies of alterations mentioned above and their patterns of repetition vary notably. In the descriptive pages, in the evocations of places and landscapes, the rhythmic order of the regular verse and strophe prevails. The passages of problematic exposition, which, in the central poem and the last three, reveal more strongly the thrust of the poet's contradictory rational tension, are those in which his rhetorical anarchy and, in a parallel fashion, his experimental intentions are manifested. The link, which can also be verified chronologically, with the proposals of the essay "La libertà stilistica" is not to be overlooked.

Chapter Seven

Teorema

The bourgeoisie from the inside

The "unresolved drama" of *Le Ceneri di Gramsci* is actively sustained by tension toward history and society. In its two versions, film and literary, *Teorema* captures the moment of "disillusionment with history" when "that attempt to maintain oneself at the high level of a reality not possessed ideologically," courageously professed in the essay "La libertà stilistica," weakens.

In the late 1960s Pasolini could find no place for himself in a neocapitalist Europe, dehumanized and corrupted by consumerism; and even less in the struggles of a student movement overly burdened, according to the author, with bourgeois implications. The existential drama assumes markedly autobiographical tones. The awareness of "diversity" is exasperated to the point of becoming an obsession, and the metaphorical extension of rejection (which underlies diversity) is inevitably projected onto the background of the indictment of the bourgeoisie and the consequent recourse to the Third World.

Thus in *Teorema,* the fundamental motifs of Pasolini's intellectual itinerary come together: his religious and social entreaties, the "disillusionment with history," the critique of the bourgeois condition as painful self-criticism and confession, and the myth of a primitive innocence existing prior to the bourgeoisie, which "has exchanged the soul for the conscience."

This chapter refers to the written work, and the author explains its genesis on the cover-leaf: "In truth, *Teorema* was born as a piece in verse, about three years ago; then it was transmuted into a film and, simultaneously, into the story the film was taken from and which the film corrected. . . ." Despite the close connection between the two versions, the book does not constitute the scenario of the film, but it clarifies the film's parable. The text cannot be precisely placed within any one literary genre. It is a series of prose statements, bare and intimately lyrical, characterized by a pace that is at once dreamy and precise, alternating with long poetic and sometimes heavily didactic insertions. Through a series of propositions which, in accordance with the Greek etymon of the title, fulfill an almost mathematical demonstrative function, *Teorema* presents the events and the consequences of the visitation by an enigmatic supernatural Guest in the midst of a typical bourgeois family. One by one, all the members of the family, and before them the servant Emilia, are physically possessed by the Guest. When at his departure, sudden and unforeseen as his arrival, the five protagonists are brutally deprived of their communion with the Guest, their reactions are dramatically different and in this difference the intended meaning of the parable is to be found.

In the first part of the book the "premises" of the theorem present the characters who, except for the maid Emilia and—up to a certain point—the paterfamilias, have a common characteristic (defined by the author as petit-bourgeois)—their inability to decide. The father is a man between forty and fifty years of age, "but very youthful . . . (his face is tanned and his hair has gone just a little gray, his body still agile and muscular, like that of a man who was athletic in his youth and continues to be so). . . . He seems to be a man deeply immersed in life: being an important man upon whom the destinies of so many other men depend has made him, as does happen, unreachable, alien, mysterious. But his mystery is, so to speak, lacking in substance and subtlety. . . ."[1]

The son Pietro "shows in his rather narrow (actually almost weak) brow the light of intelligence of one who has not lived a useless adolescence in a very rich Milanese family . . . but much more visibly than the father he has suffered from it: so that instead of coming out of it a self-assured young man, perhaps athletic like his father, he turned out to be weak, with a low purplish brow . . . already worn out by his future as a middle-class man destined not to struggle. . . ."[2] Odetta, Pietro's younger sister, is enigmatically "sweet and disquieting," but crushed "by the hurtful, masked awareness of her own nothingness. . . ."[3] Lucia, the mother, is "bored," devoted to her "sedentary" fate and to the "cult of beauty." Nonetheless, she is not without "enlightened intelligence, on a background that remains instinctively reactionary."[4]

"The family is gathered together eating, and Emilia is serving them. Emilia is an ageless girl . . . from the north of Italy; a poor rejected member of the white race. . . ."[5]

The exposition of the "data" of the theorem ends with the presentation, quite enigmatic and suspenseful, of the Guest: "Extraordinary first of all for his beauty: a beauty so exceptional as to be in almost scandalous contrast with the others present . . . socially mysterious, though he fits in perfectly well with all the others around him. . . ."[6]

The fascinated characters give themselves up to their splendid visitor. The carnal rite assumes new perspectives from one case to the next, but it maintains a basic sense of generous, almost motherly protection on the part of the Guest.

The "corollaries" following the announcement of the visitor's departure present the unraveling of the family. Mother, son, and daughter can bring to fruition neither their newly acquired awareness of their own "emptiness" nor the "knowledge" come from the Guest, and they stray along false paths. The story of the humble maid Emilia parallels that of the industrialist father. Pasolini certainly intended to indicate these parallels by the arrangement of the "data," the entries in the Appendix, and the "corollaries" relating to the characters within the text. The sub-proletariat servant returns in the bus of the poor to her home village in Lombardy where, a self-consecrated saint, she begins to perform miracles for the humble people like herself. The father, who as a character is set apart from the others from the beginning by his rational preoccupation, strips himself of his clothing and his factory (which he gives to the workers) and barely touches redemption, though he remains excluded from it because, in the final analysis, "anything a bourgeois does is wrong. . . ."[7]

I have already mentioned the fact that in *Teorema* for the first time the author describes the bourgeoisie from the inside, and his "autobiographical hatred" leads him to express himself in a judgmental manner. The anti-bourgeois polemic in this book thus assumes that trace of conventionality that one might expect, but remains sufficiently problematical to give rise to a number of interpretations, ranging from the social to the religious, moral, ideological, and even psychoanalytical.

It is neither *Teorema*'s narrative "medium" (to which I intend to return) nor the novelty of its situation, nor its psychoanalytical background that makes the book unique among Pasolini's works. It is of central importance rather as a summation of motifs. In the words of Gian Carlo Ferretti, Pasolini "moves here along the torn edge between nature and history recurring in all his works: a reincarnated mythology of the preindustrial, peasant world (now embodied in the Third World) and a vision of an immutable bourgeois history and nature; evangelical, visceral 'religion' as opposed to the capitalist industrial world, and bourgeois 'reason' now reduced to the desperate necessity of self-definition, of 'knowing what it is.' "[8] To Ferretti's words I should like to add that the text of *Teorema* elaborates and synthesizes Pasolini's entire thematics of the 1960s. In the works of that decade one may in fact glimpse an unsuppressible aspiration, becoming ever more taut and strained, toward an Absolute that is as essential as it is unknowable. In this sense *Teorema* is of primary importance: Its philosophical connotation is that of an uncompromising idealism. The dominating force is the anxiety of "intuition," if we wish to use Bergson's definition; or of "transcendental apperception" in a Kantian sense; or of Schopenhauer's "Will." The process of approach is so irrational (as suits the poet?) that the whole itinerary of the romantic experience can be helpful in analyzing this extemporaneous product of anguished spiritualism.

From the point of view of expressive medium, one need only think of the "desert," the fundamental element and dimension in *Teorema* (and not just according to psychoanalytical interpretation) beginning with the biblical quotation that introduces the text: "But God led the people about, through the way of the wilderness" (Exodus 13:18)[9] to the prolix symbolical interpretation: "The Oneness of the desert was like a dream. . . . One was the desert, and One was a step further; One two steps further; One for all the steps the Hebrews could take . . ."[10] to the many quotations throughout the entire narration, which constitute its leit-motif and are in counterpoint with the stages of this exemplary story, stressing its eternity: "single form" and as such "always omnipresent as well"; "prehistoric form of loneliness"; "visual form of the absolute."

Furthermore, Pasolini's spirit is by nature Christian; that is to say, he must bring to account the experience and conditioning of Catholicism, if not simply the archetype of Mediator-Savior-Demiurge present in all religions, positive and otherwise: At this point the figure of the mysterious Guest and the chance of redemption he offers to the bourgeois family enter in. The idea that, in general terms, the road to the Divine passes through a sexual dimension is anything but new to one who is familiar with the psychology of religion and the history of rituals.

The palingenetic and cathartic element of sexuality in *Teorema* has the same significance as cannibalism (Pasolini seems to be gradually rediscovering the entire repertory of ritual) will have in *Porcile,* where the main character, captured and condemned by a scandalized society, proclaims the famous line: "I have eaten my father and my mother and I tremble with joy!" That is, awareness is achieved by the overcoming of the existential condition of carnal filiation (in psychoanalytic terms, the overcoming of the birth trauma of separation).

In Hebrew terminology specifically, "knowledge" connoting physical union symbolizes the achievement of global contact with reality. Pasolini's quotation of a passage from the book of Jeremiah in the "Enclosures" to *Teorema* facilitates our reading of the symbols: "O Lord, thou hast deceived me; and I was deceived; thou art stronger than I, and hast prevailed [also in a physical sense]: I am in derision daily, every one mocketh me" (Jeremiah 20:7).[11]

Many of the attributes of the arcane figure of the Guest are derived from the religious inventory: the Revealer, Innocence, the Destroyer, the Adorable One. Others, mentioned above, denote heavily physical characteristics. On the whole, the identity of the mysterious Visitor seems to be without precise philosophical implications: All the elements of the parable, not to mention the basic allegorical sense, make him rather the "mediator" of an authenticity that is primitive and instinctual spontaneity of being. The Guest is the hypothetical means to a life marked by absolute fidelity to one's own nature, prior to any moralistic social conditioning. The miracle consists in his offer to the bourgeois of a chance to recover this state of primitive innocence and human dignity. At the disappearance of the Guest, everyone finds himself alone with the privilege of a truth too pitiless and radical to be lived, except by the maid Emilia. She belongs to this rural sub-proletariat world which, like the Friuli of his childhood and adolescence, is assumed by the poet to be the mythic receptacle of sacredness. Emilia returns to this world and its religious peace, and her miracles are the proof of her identification with the arcane forces of nature.

The bourgeois father, Paolo, is spared at least in part from the total devastation that sweeps away the other members of the family. He is the "mature adult male," the one who does not "lose or betray God,"[12] the most spiritual member of the family. In him we recognize the close presence of the author. The only one of the family not to have yielded to instinct without thinking, he is also the one who comes the closest to salvation. He gives the factory away to his workers and, in the large, crowded station of Milan, strips off all his clothing. The renunciation of material possessions, motivated not by love but by a sense of guilt, cannot guarantee his salvation. Salvation for him appears when, finally naked on the sand of a desert both eternal and new, he utters the "cry" of one who, at the limit of annihilation, finally "knows":

> È un urlo che vuol far sapere,
> in questo luogo disabitato, *che io esisto,*
> oppure, che non soltanto esisto,
> *ma che so.* È un urlo
> in cui in fondo all'ansia
> si sente qualche vile accento di speranza;
> oppure un urlo di certezza, assolutamente assurdo,
> dentro a cui risuona, pura, la disperazione. . . .[13]
>
> It is a cry that would make known
> in this uninhabited place, *that I exist,*
> or else, that I not only exist,
> *but that I know.* It is a cry
> where in the depths of anguish
> there is some vile accent of hope;
> or rather a cry of certainty, absolutely absurd,
> where there resounds, pure, despair. . . .

The meaning of this unseemly bestial "cry," which shook the spectators of the film and was interpreted in the most imaginative ways, could express the newly acquired awareness that—in order to "know" and "exist"—the stripping away of clothing and factories is not enough. One must be naked not in symbol, but in reality.

Thus the bourgeois father has managed to bring his "knowledge" to fruition and to touch redemption, while the others, son, daughter, and wife, "betray" and remain hopelessly cast out.

Identification of Incest with Reality

It is at this point that the interpretive resources of psychoanalysis (taken on by Pasolini as a new dimension of knowledge, although at a rather elementary level) become indispensable. Characteristic of all the Visitor's couplings with the various members of the bourgeois family is the prefiguration of incest. Within psychoanalysis, incest is a typical ingredient of salvation, an obligatory element of the process of overcoming the Oedipal complex by going backwards, "killing the primordial father again" and recovering the purity and freedom of Being.

The father and mother recognize their son in the Guest; the son and daughter see him as brother and father. Through incest, therefore, every member of the family receives the revelation of his own most intimate nature. However, at the Guest's departure each one falls back into the lack of authenticity of his or her previous experience, and the new emptiness is only the clearer and more distressing.

The poetic passages which, like a series of explanatory monologues, make up the Appendix of the first part of the book, become extremely important for the interpretation of this particular level of the narrative. Here the autobiographical element emerges with cruel evidence. In the case of Pietro we learn that his contact with the Visitor has revealed to the boy his "diversity." The acceptance of this truth, which is the transfiguration of "diversity" as awareness of the separation as an individual, is shadowed by fear and the inability to live it to the full: "It is the awareness of loss/ that gives me the awareness of my diversity. . . . Was it your intention/ perhaps to push me onto the road of diversity/ to the full and without compromise?. . . And you have been a father without wrinkles and gray hair,/ . . . Could not a father like this one/ replace you? Even if/ that is inconceivable and frightening,/ or rather, just because of that?"[14]

The truth is too harsh and radical for Pietro, like Odetta or Lucia, to resolve to live by it completely. The young man leaves his home and family circle and falls into a sudden, rabid devotion to an abstractly mechanical form of art. His awareness of the mystifying randomness of his performance almost obviously brings us back to the heart of anti-avant-garde polemic, without excluding, once again, a deep autobiographical matrix: "We must invent new techniques—unrecognizable ones—that don't resemble any previous operation. . . . Make up one's own world, with which no comparison is possible, for which there exists no preceding standard of judgment. The standards must be new, like the technique. No one must realize that the author isn't worth anything, that he is an abnormal, inferior being. . . . Everything must be presented as perfect, based on *rules that are unknown,* and therefore cannot be judged. . . ."[15]

Odetta ("What do you want to suggest and propose mysteriously to me?/ Perhaps someone who could take your place?/ And this someone could be someone/ who, like you, takes for me the place of my father,/ Pietro's father, the First Father?/ And why not my father himself, for that matter?/ Maybe you want to suggest that to me . . . the identification within one truth/ ever unimaginable and incestuous,/ with the whole of reality?")[16] expresses her refusal to live, in her choice of an obstinate madness. Her doggedly clenched fist, which will not open, is another evident Freudian symbol.

Lucia, the mother, will seek the "truth" revealed to her by the Guest in the experience of empty, degrading sexual dissipation: "What do you want to push me into?/ . . . Perhaps you want to tell me, boy that you are, that it is possible/ to replace your body and your soul/ with the body and soul of a boy who resembles you?/ . . . And why, if he must be the age of my son/ . . . why not my son himself?"[17] She too, finally, evades the necessary choice in the easy consolation of a little country church, filled with all the cherished sentimental attributes of traditional religion.

The deliberateness of *Teorema*'s narrative structure is reaffirmed on this level in Emilia's "corollaries." There should remain no doubt that the sub-proletariat constitutes Pasolini's ideological and sentimental weakness. Since Emilia, by virtue of being a member of the sub-proletariat, is outside history, she has no need of the regenerative "trauma." By a real intervention of a deus ex machina, she need not travel the hazardous road of self-recognition: She is already an immediate candidate for salvation, even sainthood, just by having encountered the Lord's Anointed, who frees her from her historical condition of slavery.

In the formal construction of the text, the conclusion of Emilia's story, in its successive phases, acts as a counterpoint to the conclusion of the other stories: The maid seated motionless on the beach, intimately involved in the process of her gradual illumination, surrounded at first by the timid curiosity of the peasants and then protected by their acceptance, is contrasted with Odetta, motionless in the bed of a luxury hospital, with her fist rigidly closed and her family around her, dully recognizing themselves in the opaque madness of the girl. The miracles finally wrought by Emilia are followed by the demonstration of Pietro's creative impotence; Lucia's sterile attempt to find refuge in the melancholy little church of the "ancient terrible religion" is followed by the confirmation of Emilia's "sainthood," her levitation, her reabsorption into the mystery of the cosmic forces.

The "corollaries" of the father, however, are placed within the structure of the text in such a way that they evidently complement Emilia's, as we have already observed. The quintessential bourgeois, who reads Tolstoy and lives his contradictions to the full, breaking with his own world and refusing authority and possessions, is the incarnation of the only alternative to salvation. Salvation eludes him because he is bourgeois: This constitutes the flagrant over-simplification upon which the allegory of *Teorema* hinges, and the self-destructive inconsistency of the author.

The stylistic components

In the first of the "Enclosures" the author indicates another fundamental direction for the reading of *Teorema:* A quotation from the "Poésies" of Rimbaud states, if ever there were any need, the allegorical function of the Guest.[18] Beyond this quotation, other and in my opinion more significant fragments of Rimbaud appear as far-from-casual sources of inspiration for Pasolini, and, besides confirming the essentially learned and artistic aspect of *Teorema,* they indicate the extent and the complexity of the interior expansion of some of the key moments of the book.

The poetic prose of "Les déserts de l'amour" presents many of the features of the encounter between the Guest and Emilia, even to the detail of her submission "with the humility of a dog" that freely echoes, on the level of context, the "je puis dire que c'était un petit chien" of the analogous situation in Rimbaud.[19] Within this tonal correspondence, all the more meaningful in that it is poetically sublimated and integrated, we must mention that "Les déserts de l'amour" concerns itself pretty directly with Rimbaud's homosexuality and betrays a raking sense of guilt.

In one of the "Illuminations" Rimbaud again writes: "A Genie appeared, of a beauty ineffable, undeclarable even. From his physiognomy and from his bearing issued the promise of a love manifold and complex! of a happiness inexpressible, insupportable even!"[20]

In other fragments of the same group, Rimbaud dreams of "a new love" which would embody spiritual and erotic bliss.[21] Quite beyond the similarities with the attributes and the cathartic function of Pasolini's Guest, it is the climax that strikes us and the poignant confessions, the analogous ambivalent vision the poets hold of themselves and the transfiguration of the existential and artistic experience of the one in that of the other.

In specifying the function of the stylistic components of *Teorema* we are once again aided by the author. In an interview by Tommaso Anzoino in 1970, speaking of his position as a novelist confronted by the linguistic problems of the "writing" of the novel, Pasolini said: "I don't think I could in all my remaining life write of the bourgeois or petit-bourgeois world; or of the world of the privileged class: I could never be mimetic in relation to it; and besides, I am not sufficiently detached and free of hatred to speak of it in pure Italian . . . (at the most I could again use the dreamy, ephemeral language of *Teorema*)."[22] Elucidating the author's words and discussing *Teorema,* Anzoino comments: "Here is the first novelty of the work: the bourgeois world. . . . This entails two big problems: the position to assume and, as a consequence, the language to use. Pasolini the 'realist' of the sub-proletariat was mimetic; now, in relation to the bourgeoisie, he cannot be . . ., therefore a 'novel' about the bourgeoisie he cannot write: he can, however, write a 'parable'. Its programmatic, allegorical nature permits him to use a neutral ('dreamy and ephemeral') language, which is limited to description: from the facts thus presented, the symbolic meaning will emerge directly."[23]

Teorema is a work in which analysis, description, and motivation dissolve in the face of the absolute relevance of facts. The text is predominantly visual; the characters are identified through the schematic precision of the "data" and the "corollaries," which assume the function that subjective focusing has in cinematographic technique. The exclusion of psychological inquiry points up the emblematic quality of the protagonists, and the verification of their basic experience is, from this point of view, evidential: The "love" of the five for the Guest is without any psychological connotation; every episode starts out *in medias res* when the respective protagonists are already hopelessly enamored of the visitor, and ends with their coupling. The Guest gives himself in carnal union with an impartial, understanding serenity that reaffirms the emblematic intention of the whole.

The aspect of the language of *Teorema* which Pasolini defined as "dreamy and ephemeral" shows that "recourse to oneirism" of the Freudian type which Michel David has found in the verses of *Poesia in forma di rosa.*[24] In *Teorema* this recourse is developed to the point of becoming a fundamental stylistic preoccupation, sometimes mechanically exhibited. The behavior of the five characters is registered through episodic nuclei unconnected by a temporal link, so that the order of presentation could be changed without changing the narrative results. The key events that presuppose even a vague "before" and "after" are the appearance of the Guest and his departure. Around these "occurrences" other "occurrences" take place, as in a dream, outside any concept of past and future, in a continuous present revealed mainly through verbal syntax, sometimes rather laboriously. We do not find in *Teorema* (or in *Poesia in forma di rosa*) psychological and poetic time substituted for the normal coordinates of succession, following the procedure of the revolution in perceptions inaugurated by the works of Marcel Proust. Nor are we aided in this matter by recourse to Rimbaud's *Illuminations,* where movement occurs in a continuing present within independent single fragments. Here as in a dream, the relation between cause and effect is expressed in occurrences, and these very occurrences, according to one of the many didactic statements in the text, "happen at the same time in the same place."[25]

The author mentions the light of day and the darkness of night, but the light or darkness of which day or night, he professes not to want to know: "(Is this evening before or after the day it happened to Emilia? It could be before or after: that has no importance.)"[26] "More time passed. (Maybe days, maybe weeks or maybe even years.)"[27] The events are placed within seasons through a purely esthetic dimension: "It is an unspecified season (it might be spring, or the beginning of autumn; or both of them together, because this story of ours has no chronological succession), and the poplars that surround the immense clearing where the factory was built (only a few months or years ago) in long, regular lines, are naked, or just beginning to bud (or else their leaves are dry)."[28] There are many such descriptive pauses, and they mark the pages of greater poetic consistency, those which transcend the substance of the proposed "code" and the informative and didactic resolution.

In constant and consistent relation to the suffering and the ideological choice of the poet, *Teorema* fits into the same literary myth, as abstract as it is individual, with his other works, but with differing expressive choices. The eternal ingredients of sexual mysticism, purifying and purified narcissism, natural religiosity filtered from time to time through popular Christian forms, or stretched to recover an absolute and ideal essentiality, are still present and pressing. Despite reservations of a general and ideological nature and those due to the heaviness of abused psychological and religious symbols, *Teorema* merits a positive judgment.

Chapter Eight
The Theater of the Word

Manifesto for a new theater

Pasolini's interest in the theater, which seems to explode with the production—in a short period of time—of six whole works, shows itself to be singularly consistent with his political and intellectual stance, and not merely because the genre presents to him an alternative to literature and the cinema, which are by now preyed upon by commercialization.

Published in the January, 1968, issue of *Nuovi Argomenti,* the "Manifesto per un nuovo teatro" [Manifesto for a new theater] is linked to Pasolini's other works, both film and literary, immediately preceding and following it, in the continuous, sustained quality of its anti-bourgeois polemic.

In one of the few analyses to date of this text, which has made its mark on the history of Italian theater, especially experimental theater, of the second half of this century, as well as on Pasolini's works, Gualtiero De Santi captures its principal motif: "The 'Manifesto' . . . sets out to demolish not only and not so much the idea the reader may have of the theater, but rather the theater of the bourgeoisie, in the permanent characteristics of its exercise . . . and in its false pretense, synonymous with 'false conscience,' of a break with the bourgeois world on the level of language."[1] Through forty-three clauses Pasolini first sets forth his indictment of both traditional theater (defined as theater of Chatter) and the more salient manifestations of avant-garde theater (defined as theater of Gesture or Howl). He accuses the latter of being opposed to the first only as a matter of form, closed and circumscribed within a rebellion that is an end in itself, incapable of rational opposition, in the reality conservative of that stage action which—by making the world ancillary to physical presence—obscures and destroys the essential nature of the drama.[2]

Proceeding, according to his custom, to clarify his argument through a series of negative statements, Pasolini analyzes the "confirmation" that constitutes the final purpose of both the theater of Chatter in the hypocrisy of its function and the theater of Gesture or Howl in its inconclusive irrationality. In the first case he finds a ritual "confirmation"—for the average audience—of its own bourgeois convictions. In the second case he recognizes an equally ritual "confirmation"—for the advanced groups who produce and enjoy underground theater in their surreptitious sophistication—of their own anti-bourgeois convictions.

Willing to exclude any prefabricated message, Pasolini thus proposes "a theater that is first of all debate, exchange of ideas, literary and political struggle," on a level "as democratic and rational as possible."[3] The new theater "to be defined, albeit tritely . . . as 'theater of the Word' "[4] requests the public to come to its performances "more with the intention of listening than of seeing (a necessary restriction in order to better understand the words you will hear, *and therefore the ideas, which are the real protagonists of this theater*)."[5]

In this theater which desires and solicits the democracy of confrontation, where ideas are the protagonists and problems are proposed and debated "with all rules suspended!"[6] conventional scenarios and the actor's personal charisma are obviously superfluous. To achieve the greatest theatrical effectiveness the text must not be contaminated by action or movement: The nucleus will rather be the monologue. Absolute space must be left for the Word alone, as a vehicle that does not require support by sensory means. The scenery will be understated to the point of squalor, to avoid its becoming the receptacle of symbols. The objects—a bench, a bed— will have only functional presence and value. There will be two or three, never more, "living vehicles" of the text who will carry out an essentially linear drama, in which stage action disappears, along with all other possible distractions, in the consummation of a "cultural rite" that brings together author, actors, and audience.

The necessity and the difficulty of identifying the intended audience of his theater escapes neither Pasolini's critical acumen nor his need for clarity and desire to provoke. In clauses 15 and 16 (which he himself will later describe as the fundamental parts of the "Manifesto")[7] the author indicates tht he addresses the theater of the Word to the "cultivated" bourgeois minority, making them the repository of its cultural function. To this minority Pasolini gives over immediate responsibility as a catalyzing agent and the role of cultural avant-garde. To prevent or counter any accusation of inherent contradiction in the hypothesis of a "new" theater, destined for "the advanced groups of the bourgeoisie," the author reminds everyone that, in political terms, the same role of avant-garde and guide for the masses of peasants and workers was reserved for the advanced intellectuals of the Bolshevik party.

In a rather summary fashion that his further statements do not entirely clarify, Pasolini then mentions the specific intermediary function that those who have a real interest in culture debate and who will be the first to enjoy his plays must take upon themselves, in order to help the masses excluded from the privilege of culture. Their task will be to re-present, in the freest possible manner and on a basic level (that is, in working places and neighborhood club-houses), the cultural rite of the new theater, without however intending to impose a packaged, defined message upon the people. If this point does not invalidate the substance of Pasolini's proposal, it is nevertheless the most ambiguous of the entire "Manifesto." De Santi comments on its "prophetic productivity": "The role of the intelligentsia thus becomes . . . the role of one who opposes his own class, remaining dialectically close to the workers' movement. When the bourgeoisie has exhausted its functions and while the people are not yet able to develop concrete proposals . . . it is the task of the anguished self-consciousness of the bourgeoisie to find temporary solutions."[8]

Pasolini himself (probably battle-trained by the controversy following the publication of the "Manifesto") punctiliously reiterates the fundamental "democratic" quality of the new theater in an article in the December 1, 1968, issue of *Il Giorno,* shortly following the presentation of *Orgia:*

"The "theater of the Word" is thus apparently aristocratic, since it imposes the selection of an intended audience, brutally excluding . . . anyone who is not in effect an intellectual at the same cultural level as the author. In reality, . . . the "theater of the Word" is democratic by its very nature, which is strictly cultural. In fact it is silly to confuse "democratic culture" with "mass culture." The "theater of the Word" . . . is totally opposed to mass culture which is terrorist, repressive, stereotyped, un-human . . . certainly anti-democratic. Theater . . . can never be a "mass medium": because theater is not reproducible, only repeatable (as in ancient Greece!), and it implies the physical presence of all those who celebrate the theatrical rite: actors and spectators. Where there are the ears and mouths of single individuals . . . *there can be no mass culture.* It is for this reason . . . that the "theater of the Word" affirms its real democracy, as opposed to the false democracy of the communications media that address the masses."[9]

Aside from and beyond the concept of the "democratic" quality of the new theater—the importance of which I nonetheless wish to stress—I am in total accord with De Santi's conclusions regarding the essentials of Pasolini's proposal:

". . . the fury of desecration . . . and the need for an almost absolute theatrical (and therefore cultural) revolution . . . And thus the provocatory insights and demands as well: the idea of a new audience, and the equally stimulating idea of its mode of existence (the actor on an equal intellectual plane with the spectator); or the very hypothesis of a dramaturgy in which ideas become the characters . . ."[10]

Orgia

It is necessary to observe that the postulates and intention of the "Manifesto" were evidently developed before 1968, and they represent the theoretical schematization of what the poet had laboriously attempted to demonstrate in his individual works. We know in fact that Pasolini had written six entire plays during the illness he suffered in 1966[11] and that the first draft of *Orgia* dates back as far as 1965. According to Pasolini's address to his first audience, the play, in the draft of 1965, was elaborated as the tragedy of the existential relationship with history. In the successive drafts it theorized sexual communication as language. Its final version was intended by the author (who specifically selected *Orgia* for performance) as a lesson in the "new" theater that would be more precise and exemplary than any theoretical declaration.[12]

Consistent with the dictates of the "Manifesto" there are only three characters, never more than two in a scene. There first appear a husband and a wife, chained to each other by a sado-masochistic relationship whose roots sink in an inextricable tangle of memories, dreams, and obsessions. While the husband prepares to bind his victim-accomplice with a rope in order to vent upon her and with her their self-destructive instincts, the two calmly and minutely discuss their abnormality. Later the wife, a contemporary, reasoning Medea, will commit suicide after killing their two children, in her desire to bring scandal to a motionless world "so that it will move and not provoke any more remorse." Left alone, the husband is led to consider his own sexual "diversity" a legitimate need for freedom, and he in his turn expresses the unsuppressible need for scandal. His reviving sadism is then turned on a poor young prostitute, who nonetheless manages to escape him—naked and terrified—when a providential crisis strikes the man down. Upon returning, he strips off his clothing to put on, piece by piece, the poor rags left behind by his victim and hangs himself in what is intended to be an extreme gesture of protest and testimony. He makes—and these are the final words of the protagonist and of the play—"good use of his death," after declaring: "The bonze is ready."

For one who approaches the work without overlooking the concrete exigencies of theatrical representation in its language and structures, if the text is analyzed in light of the "Manifesto," several contradictions become apparent. Action is not at all eliminated: *Orgia* appears in fact to be a play based on the word (prevalently lyrical) but in order to progress, it proposes violence, and this in turn entails action. The sado-masochistic relationship is worked out in repeated manifestations of violence on the part of the man, first against his wife, then against the young prostitute. Action is entailed in the prostitute's strip-tease, the man's fainting fit, the flight of the second victim, and again in the re-awakening of the man who, after taking off his clothes, puts on those left behind by the woman, one by one. Resolving action is finally entailed in the man's suicide by hanging.

The six episodes of the play are articulated around a series of long monologues. The dialogue does not constitute the primary structure of dramatic action; it rather provides the indispensable questions that allow the monologue to start or to continue:

Man: Tell me first: where did all this happen?
Woman: In your own village.
Man: A town full of lanes white with dust?
And those trees tht no longer exist, the mulberries?

Where the blades of wheat were segments sovereign over the hours,
shall we say, of refugees come back up through Dalmatia
and Catalonia, from regions bathed by the sea?
And where, finally, the bells
trembled like nests of serpents under ground,
and the cottages sank between a willow and an acacia,
and in the center, green, radiant with sunlight, the mulberry?

In my opinion it is mainly the fact that *Orgia* (like all Pasolini's other theatrical works) was written in the language of poetry, where the word is used in its highest moment of linguistic and expressive precision, that guarantees the function of the word itself. If dramatic writing in verse does not constitute a novelty even for this century (one thinks, for instance, of Gabriele D'Annunzio and T.S. Eliot), there is no doubt that verse confers a tragic dimension on the three sadly contemporary characters of *Orgia.* Moreover, a determinant value is assumed by the evocation, the descriptive lingerings, the many repetitions, and the rhythm derived from them.

According to the "Manifesto," the word should, in its turn, propose ideas, the real protagonists of the theater inaugurated by Pasolini.

To those who criticized him because—once again—the theme of sex was preponderant, Pasolini replied in the article cited above that the problem of sex is an important one because it acts as the "vehicle" of other problems: religious, social, political, etc. According to the author, therefore, in *Orgia* the tragedy of sex, within which the two main characters destroy themselves, constitutes only the first level of representative evidence, implying, on a deeper level, the tragedy of those who are "different." As such, it involves wider categories, affirming an aspiration to a freedom naturally opposed to any manifestation of power.

If in the author's intention the man did "make good use of his death," the meaning of the protest intended to identify sexual "diversity" with that of other oppressed peoples, from Blacks to Jews, presents a lapse of logic that is difficult to surmount:

Man: . . . I, as far as my conscience is concerned
have thus accepted it, the world!
I, I've bowed my head! . . .
My will to be normal
finally doesn't count:
this is what was written and I didn't want to read. . . .
I have undergone the process of being
something *Different*. This happened to me.
By what design of the world?
So that others, maybe, would see they were right?
. . . .
But the man upon whom falls, from God, the fate
of being *Different*
must he keep still all his life,
marked, catalogued, within his difference?
Is it only for others . . .
the prerogative of going forward, that is to say
evolving and making history?
While for me, the *Different one* and all
my hapless companions in misfortune
(Blacks, Jews), nothing. No History.
A fate of immobility preserved by hatred.
By the hatred, I say, of the brothers,
who, through evolutions and revolutions,
moral and religious, go forward, little by little. . . .[14]

The different one cries out his revolt, but it is undeniable that the monologue that conditions the tragedy proclaims a "diversity" that is mainly individual. Social and political "diversity" appear to be deliberately and artificially superimposed. Consequently, sex is not the vehicle of other problems, but rather "the problem" and, perhaps beyond the author's intentions, it constitutes the content of the drama.

Other themes are, inevitably, the longing for a far-away era and the ever-beloved peasant universe, and the call of an ancient world opposed to the constrictions of the present day:

Man: . . . In moments like this
I have yearnings, like dreams
dreamt long ago
that return in the form of real things. . . .
. . . And I remember that the poplars
were sparse—green on greener grass—
And theirs was a crown of gray
around the love of the sweet peasant monkeys,
who never looked at the sky but to pray. . . .
the whole rest of the time they looked at the sod.
So they were made of wet earth and white stone,
with their hands together, and a rake in their fist. . . .[15]

Nor is fondness for the sub-proletariat absent; it is represented here by the consumptive young prostitute, "the daughter of poor folks," whom the sadist pities before he tortures her.

Pasolini's experiment as the first "lesson" of the "theater of the Word" is certainly remarkable in the sum of its parts. However, *Orgia* takes the form of an eminently literary work: a poem for three voices, objectively difficult, rich in suggestions and lyrical intimations, but without real internal progression, and fatally not articulated for representation. We must hope that the critical edition of all the texts written by Pier Paolo Pasolini for the theater will be published without further delay. Within such a context *Orgia* would find a plausible placement as the first evidence of the author's attempt to characterize the primary elements of theatrical practice and to reaffirm a "popular" theater of social and civic commitment in an era of evasive experimentalism.

Chapter Nine
Dismal Enthusiasm

A new youth

His problematic encounter with the events of 1968 would prove to be a major turning point of Pasolini's itinerary. Echoes of the student revolts can be found in all the works written or elaborated after 1968. As we have already observed, *Teorema* (and its film version), *Trasumanar e organizzar,* and *Calderón* probe deeply into the institutions (ethical, political, and cultural, respectively) in which the crisis of bourgeois society and its superstructures is building up. The mythical opposition of "nature" and "history" is not exhausted; but the poet, having denied himself even the refuge of dreams (see *Calderón*), is now obliged to record the irreversible changes involving even those absolutes in which he had at first placed his hopes for salvation: the peasant universe, the urban sub-proletariat, and finally the uncontaminated preserve of the Third World.

The true, painful novelty of the 1970s is that the polemic rejection of the present led Pasolini to conceive of an irresistible degradation of popular and humanistic values that would invest even the past. Speaking of his heroes of yesterday, Pasolini wrote in 1975:

> If those who were thus and so *then* could *now* become thus and so, it means that they were already potentially so: therefore even the way they were *then* is invalidated by the present. The children and youths of the Roman sub-proletariat . . . if they are *now* human garbage, it means that even *then* they had the potential of being so: they were therefore idiots forced to be adorable, squalid criminals, compelled to be likeable rascals, cowardly good-for-nothings compelled to be piously innocent, etc. etc.[1]

With his customary precision, Gian Carlo Ferretti observes: "[Pasolini] expresses a deeply felt rejection of the happy and miserable myth of the sub-proletariat (which had been his own), that cannot help arising from his capacity, contradictory though it be, for a touching re-examination of his own past, and from the defeat of his own world of origin. . . ."[2]

This crisis of individualization was developing into a sort of intellectual and moral schizophrenia for Pasolini: He no longer recognizes himself in youth—in "the youth"; he is no longer able either to love or to believe, since all hope of reciprocation was lost. Thus, after the "best youth," only the "new youth" is left, yearned after as in the legend of Faust while the poet pathetically reiterates: "It is not I who am old, but the world that is old," and is now unable to find the dear perennial image of Narcissus in the "dried up" spring. Naturally—psychologically—the betrayal is all on the other side, on the side of the image—different and unknowable—now facing him, and upon which he bestows the connotations of stupidity, conformity, and violence. At this particular moment the dominating figure of the interlocutor assumes the political and cultural countenance of the homogenized masses, without social or racial distinction.

In order to reach an understanding of the late Pasolini, it would be necessary to follow his advice and attempt a cross-reading (or re-reading) of *Scritti corsari* and other essays, with those poems written in Italian and Friulian which, although included in the collection *La nuova gioventù* under the generic title *Tetro entusiasmo* [Dismal enthusiasm], are for many reasons a unit in themselves, thoroughly conclusive.[3]

Consequently, an analysis of the last poetic compositions of Pier Paolo Pasolini will constitute the subject-matter of this chapter, and frequent references will be made to his essays.

The theme of the redefinition of and confrontation with the maternal-Friulian myth had gradually been done away with in the course of the rewriting in counterpoint of the first poems. I would say that the myth had consumed itself in the course of this singular operation, in a desperate historical present:

> Da la Domènia al Lunis
> dutis li erbis del mond
> si son seciadis.[4]

(From Sunday to Monday, all the grass of the world has dried up.)

An ancient treasure has been lost, squandered in a few years—from Sunday to Monday—the years of triumphant consumerism.

The opening toward a consciously political problematics will strain the expressiveness of dialect from now on. First we notice frequent interruptions of Italianisms. Then—notably in the more forcefully polemic compositions—Italian takes over. The poem "Versi buttati giù in fretta" [Verses jotted down in a hurry], castigating the Communist intellectuals' fear of opposing the system and their unchanging lack of interest in the people, is exemplary in this respect:

> They cannot see
> the transformation
> of the workers, because
> they have no interest whatever in the workers.
>
> . . . But it wrings
> my heart
> to see the fear
> of the Communist intellectuals
> to be just a bit,
> or just ideally, disobedient.
>
> They look with dismay
> mixed with admiration or hatred
> at the one who dares say something opposed
> to the institutionalized opposition.
> I wonder what they're afraid of.
> Is it the ancient fear
> of being left behind by the herd?[5]

In "Versi sottili come righe di pioggia" [Verses slender as lines of rain] the analogy with the motifs already—or concurrently—developed in *Scritti corsari* becomes more explicit and direct, in the invective against the banality of progressivism, laicism, and the false rationality which have corrupted the innocence of the people. Every now and then, there wearily resurfaces the purely sentimental nostalgia for boys as they used to be, in their childish, innocent corruption, and with "short hair." Only death saves them. In the poem "Salerno," where Pasolini speaks of a young bandit killed by the police in Rome in 1974, verses in Friulian alternate with verses in Italian: "Poor face of a bandit, or rather of a child. . . . They chose a pretty, dark-skinned lad, with short hair. The Son. The Man. The Poor. . . . His companions who stayed alive, on the other hand, are ugly. Ugly as the police that killed him. . . ."[6]

In *Scritti corsari,* symbolic physical mutation becomes the object of a polemic and political disquisition. The poet speaks of Isfahan ". . . in the heart of Persia. An underdeveloped country, as they so horribly say, but as they equally horribly say, in full take-off. . . . In its streets, at work, or taking a walk toward evening, you see the boys you saw in Italy ten years ago: dignified, humble children, with their pretty napes and beautiful clear faces under proud, innocent forelocks. And here one evening, walking along the main street, I saw, among all those ancient boys, beautiful and full of the ancient human dignity, two monstrous beings . . . their hair was cut European style, long in back . . . with two disgusting locks over the ears. What did that hair say? It said: 'We do not belong to the number of these starvelings, these poor underdeveloped wretches, left back in the Stone Age! . . . We are city folk: and here is our long hair to prove how modern and international and privileged we are!' . . . It has come full cycle. The subculture in power has absorbed the subculture of the opposition and has made it its own. . . ."[7]

In the last essays as in the last poems, beside the indignation sometimes expressed in violent and provocatory accents, we detect the indications of a renewed tension, opened to a more vital, more fruitful confrontation with a world that remains the enemy. Let us consider first of all the title of the group of poems concluding *La nuova gioventù,* "Dismal enthusiasm." Here, in the easy example of the oxymoron, one finds on the one hand a reminder of the macabre nihilism of *Salò.* However, in the poems, especially in those that might seem less remarkable from the standpoint of poetic results (and the pages that are soberly and fully lyrical are rather few), the motif of "turning back" assumes new color and a new, darkly enthusiastic dimension. Beyond the salvaging of the myth of innocent poverty, the change invoked seems radical, in its desire to bring about a "tabula rasa":

Thus we can no longer go *forward*. We will have to turn *back*, and start again from the beginning. So that our children will not be educated by the bourgeois, so that our souls will not be tempted by the bourgeoisie. Because, if our culture cannot and must not be any longer the culture of poverty (a peasant, proletariat, paleo-industrial culture; a special culture, a dialectal culture), it must be transformed into a communist culture. . . . Let us turn *back*, with clenched fists, and let us start again from the beginning.[8]

In the poem "La recessione," the outlining—in dialect—of a blissfully regressive culture caused by the economic recession that struck Italy in the early 1970s, is bluntly interrupted by a final admonition in Italian: "But enough of this neo-realistic film/ We have sworn off what it represents./ Re-experiencing it only makes sense/ if we will fight for a truly Communist world."[9] Here the bristling polemic and the anxiety to begin again, this time in a drastically new way, break the circle of the regressive myth.

As I have already mentioned, the ending of *Salò* is as enigmatic as it is possibly emblematic of hope if we remember the reference to the fiancée of one of the two young men whose dance ends the nightmare: ". . . Yes, and her name is Margaret." The final verses (in Friulian) of the last composition of *Tetro entusiasmo* attenuate the weariness of the poem:

> . . . E jo i ciaminarai
> lizèir, zint avant, sielzínt par sempri
> la vita, la zoventút.[10]

(And I shall walk lightly, going forward, choosing forever life and youth.)

It is not given us to know up to what point we are justified in talking of an opening, of a polemic reawakening, of the confused beginning of a new phase in Pasolini's thought and how the characteristics of this new phase of the poet's experience would develop; for—if it existed—it was cut off by his death.

In fact, in the "Abiura dalla *Trilogia della vita*" [Abjuration from

The Trilogy of life], written late in 1975, we are presented with a man who has finally and clearly overcome the myth of the past, but who is also, and above all, imprisoned in the ruins of the present, adapting himself to degradation. The existential position of the last Pasolini is too complex and unsettled to give rise to definitive judgments and interpretations, and the contradictions are exasperated and radicalized by the poet's unsolved, tragic end.

The last poem

There remains to be analyzed, in light of the political and existential conclusions reached by the poet—as far as we can tell—in the 1970s, his declaredly last poem in Friulian, "Saluto e augurio" [Greetings and best wishes], the poem which closes *Tetro entusiasmo* and with it, *La nuova gioventù*. Pasolini intended it to be a poem-testament: "I vuèj fati un discors/ ch'al somèa a un testamínt."[11] (I want to make you a speech that seems like a testament.)

The role of an old man, as opposed to the eternal search for an uncorrupted, vital youth, certainly marks the passage to a phase of moral and intellectual lassitude, a sort of definitive refusal to understand, to interpret, to polemicize. In fact, Pasolini, with the publication of the articles and essays now collected in *Scritti corsari* and *Lettere luterane,* had entered into the thick of political and sometimes literary controversy, dealing with and debating themes of the greatest actuality (from the referendum on divorce to the problems of the schools and universities, from abortion to the situation of homosexuals in Italy, to the latest books published).[12] It is equally true, however, that the poet's polemic against neocapitalism, begun in 1950, becomes rigid and obdurate in its repeated denunciations of the hedonism of consumer society, the leveling of the classes, the moral and social repressiveness of the Christian Democratic régime—without any offering of possible alternatives, even mythical ones.

The message of "Saluto e augurio" is the message "of sleep": "Your shirt [that of the young interlocutor] should be gray. The shirt of sleep."[13] "Saluto e augurio" is also "testamental," and therefore conclusive, as regards the Friulian dialect and universe. I have already observed that *La nuova gioventù* marks both the last confrontation (Pasolini had returned to the Friuli after years of absence) with the origins of the maternal myth and the bitter ascertainment of its illusory nature, through lucid correction and often desecration of the semantic values of the tender, lyrical language of the first poems.

Tetro entusiasmo abandons these themes for a more precisely political and up-to-date discussion. With those themes, the dialect is forsaken as an inadequate tool for the polemic, discursive tones and moments. The Friulian dialect is needed again, however, in the last composition, which expresses a further evocation of the fields, the farmhouses, the meadows, in order to make a definitive assessment of the possible "present-day" meaning of such a world.

The attitude is obviously no longer that of an irresponsible mythical regression, nor of a fond, heartfelt nostalgia. The bitter desecration of the myth is equally far from the poet's intentions. His is, basically, an emotionally detached position, and therefore a more balanced one—in a sense, more realistic as well. Against an industrialized, consumerist, centralized society that has inexorably absorbed the peripheral and peasant cultures without integrating them, the only tactic is a defense and preservation; strenuous, "saintly," or "soldierly" defense of the land and the peasant values: "Defend the stake of mulberry, of alder, in the name of the gods, Greek or Chinese. Die of love for the vineyards. For the figs in the garden. The stumps, the twigs. . . . Defend the fields between the town and the country, with their abandoned corn-cobs. Defend the meadows between the last house in town and the fosse. . . . Defend, preserve, pray!"[14] This is the message from the poet to his interlocutor.

The motif of defense and preservation thus dissolves into the creation of a new myth that shows the effects of Pasolini's spiritual weariness, as it shows the persistence of the cult of maternal values: "Defend, preserve, pray! The Republic is within the body of the mother. The fathers have sought and sought again, here and there, being born, dying, changing: but they are all things of the past."[15] Thus on one side there are the fathers, who are indeed the father-masters and usurpers of all time, but who also symbolize a dialectic of movement and struggle as well as searching.[16] On the other side there impends the static quality and the position of implicit renunciation of the maternal values, with the archetypal mother who watches over and cares for what is finished and done with, who represents passivity and the instinct of preservation, who once again beckons toward the inertia and rest of the womb. Furthermore, the cyclic, natural, feminine scansion of time, marked by the recurring seasons and religious celebrations, is opposed to the historical tension of the vigil: "Do hate those who want to wake up and forget about Easter."[17]

Pasolini's discourse in this poem is openly religious as well, with a "new" religiosity that is more a call back to the sacredness of the institutions and values of the past, of the divinities of family and field, than a provocatory, heterodox message. The anarchist Christ of the *Vangelo secondo Matteo* is no longer invoked, but rather "the King, the Right Hand of God who is within us, in our sleep."[18] The call back to the Commandments and the Church as an institution is specific, in an attempt to reaffirm the soundness of the "roots" that must be defended against every assault of the new: "There where you were born. There where as a child you learned their Commandments. But in the City? There Christ is not enough. You need the Church. . . ."[19]

The poet's attitude, always severely critical of the Catholic Church because of its connivance with Christian Democratic power and its heavily bureaucratic structure (cf. *San Paolo*), tends in the later writings to direct itself toward a denunciation of the weakness of the Church, unable to oppose to the strength of its dogmas and traditions the lay "neo-hedonism" of consumer society. At this point, the term *laicism* assumes a negative connotation in Pasolini's vocabulary, as a synonym for the loss or mutilation of values and "sacred" traditions: "Such laicism is a 'new value' born in bourgeois entropy, in which religion is wasting away as an authority and a form of power, and survives only in that it is still a natural product of enormous consumption and a folk tradition that can still be exploited."[20]

The relaunching of the Church as an institution is the basis for the outraged polemic against the tolerance of the official religious institutions for the publicity for "Jesus" jeans,[21] and touches on the themes of divorce and abortion (against which "solutions" Pasolini expressed a negative view), finally assuming the tones of a "crusade":

Once again taking up a struggle that is in any case a part of its tradition (the struggle of the Papacy against the Empire), but not for the conquest of power, the Church could be the guide, prominent but not authoritarian, of all those who reject (and it is a Marxist who speaks, just because he is a Marxist) the new consumerist power that is completely irreligious; totalitarian; violent; falsely tolerant, nay, more repressive than ever; corrupting; degrading (never more than today had Marx's affirmation that capital transforms human dignity into a commodity of exchange had more meaning). It is this rejection that the Church could symbolize, returning to its origins, that is to opposition and revolt.[22]

The alternatives proposed to the Church are two: either return to being a strong, powerful, secure institution, the representative on earth of the "King, the Right Hand of God," or disappear altogether, fleeing both the opprobrium of consumerist degradation and especially a position of false modernity and tolerance on a moral level.

After the severe hymn to the Church, "Saluto e augurio" proceeds to take up again, one by one, the motifs dear to the poet, to redefine them. After the countryside and the religion of the humble, Pasolini reintroduces the city with its poor and its sub-proletariat masses. Even in the city the poor man is seeking shelter in a position of "defense," intent on tracing out a barrier against every assault and outside help. In this case it is not a matter of tangible territorial boundaries between the field and the town, between the last house and the irrigation ditch, but rather, within the urban leveling and uniformity, of linguistic barriers: ". . . *do* love their diversity. Love their will to live alone in their world, among meadows and mansions, where no word of our world comes; love the boundaries that have been marked between us and them; love the dialect invented every morning so as not to be understood, not to share their mirth with anyone. . . ."[23]

If the people living beyond the boundaries of history symbolize the poet's myth to the end, the anti-bourgeois polemic with its active and ever-renewed tension finally ceases because the leveling performed by the establishment of well-being and consumerism has homologized the Italians. The old social distinctions no longer exist and the goals and aspirations are the same for all. Within a classless society, the dialectic of class struggle no longer makes sense. "Believe in the bourgeois man who is blind with honesty . . . it is enough that the feeling of life be the same for everyone: the rest does not matter."[24] The poet's message is deceitfully and ironically humanitarian, just as the contemporary bourgeois establishment is only apparently tolerant of differences; in reality it represses, at the moment that it assimilates and equalizes.

Pasolini's position in the face of such a reality hides an ever more dangerous confusion between the various levels of the Italian political-ideological dispute (even if it reveals a tendency that does in fact exist): ". . . the old paleo-industrial bourgeoisie is giving way to a new bourgeoisie that understands the working class more and more deeply, tending finally to identify the bourgeoisie with humanity."[25]

Not only that: The dictatorship of consumerist society is viewed as a "new" form of Fascism more dangerous than historical Fascism, inasmuch as it hides and permits the continuation of the old and new Power:

> I believe, I believe it deeply, that the true Fascism is what the sociologists have too kindheartedly called the "consumer society." . . . If one observes reality well, and especially if he can read within objects, the countryside, town planning, and especially men, he sees that the results of this thoughtless consumer society are the results of a true Fascist dictatorship. . . . At that time [during the epoch of historical Fascism] the young people, at the very moment they were taking off their uniforms and setting out on the road toward their villages and fields, were going back to being the Italians of fifty or a hundred years before, like before Fascism. It is no longer a case, as in Mussolini's time, of a superficial, stage-like regimentation, but rather of a real regimentation that has stolen away and changed the souls. . . . So if the word *Fascism* means the arrogance of power, the "consumer society" has well realized Fascism. . . .[26]

Mussolini's Fascism, therefore, as a rhetorical mask, had not scratched the essence of a popular world where "smile and poverty" blended to give substance to the existence and culture of the sub-proletariat. Through the "defense" of the traditional values of the family and religion, and of a robust simplicity of habits, the earlier Fascism had even permitted the survival of the irreplaceable values of the popular, peasant universe. It had been, in a sense, a "better Fascism." This conclusion epitomizes the singularity and also the paradox of Pasolini's argument, an argument that assumes decisive proportions and resonances because it was his last. Out of respect to the writer, as much as for the necessity of critical interpretation, this argument must be examined closely.

It emerges as a basic political conception in *Scritti corsari,* a very complex and magmatic work, since it is a group of "interventions" and therefore anything but organic.[27] In my view, the limitation of the "Corsair" writings and therefore of the conclusions one might draw from them, lies in the tendency—inevitably transmitted from Pasolini to his readers—to broaden certain analyses, in themselves perspicacious but limited, into an all-inclusive system. Such a system, loaded with basic contradictions of largely subjective origin, shows the attempt to subordinate the whole to the elementary exposition of the "physical glory" inherent in things.

The "consumer society" has, in truth, literally eaten up the old agrarian world, intensifying the formation of a rural proletariat bearing a vision of relationships different from the inherited one based on stability, the discipline of obedience, and finally the recognized characteristics of resignation. The values of rustic mythology have been subverted. Acculturation has, in truth, destroyed a large part of the real culture. Within this acculturation, however, the masses—including the peasants—have acquired a new political awareness, both on the collective and the individual level.

Pasolini's conclusions relating to a political and historical situation that for thirty years (now thirty-five) had seen the Christian Democrats as the determining factor of a basic structural continuity from pre-Fascism and Fascism itself, are, on the other hand, penetrating and indisputable.

The essay entitled "L'articolo delle lucciole" [The article of the fireflies] presents "before and after the disappearance of the fireflies" the investigation of a society in which democracy is only apparent and hedonism takes the shape of false freedom, since it is a totalitarianism descending from above, rather than individual acquisition of liberties. In this essay, tied to the Friulian poetry by the felicitous metaphor of the fireflies vanished from the fields where the rivers are no longer clear, the ecological evaluation ascertains an established fact, placing it, however, completely outside the social structure.

It is the face of this metaphorical Fascism that respected the fireflies, of a provincial Fascism, vaguely academic but healthy and respectful of tradition, set in a mythical time and dissociated from reality, that Pasolini seeks in his young interlocutor of the poem "Saluto e augurio." The decision to address a young Fascist and to entrust to him a message that is, as I have already observed, in many ways conclusive, is a provocatory one and, within the Italian political scene at the beginning of the 1970s, in the midst of the ambiguous polemics over opposing extremisms, characteristically nonconformist. Once again Pasolini challenges a taboo and a truism of contemporary Italy: In order to isolate the Fascists, it is necessary not to communicate with them. In his last and extreme provocation, Pasolini chooses a paradoxical encounter with the "diversity" of reaction, of conservatism, of obedience. The weight and central importance of the choice are stressed on the cover of the volume *La nuova gioventù*, which shows the poet when he was very young, in the uniform of the "Young Fascists."

This is also, however, the logical consequence of the argument about the young people of today and about cultural leveling. Within a polemic against a generation superficially committed to protest against the system, but in reality assimilated to consumerist values, it makes no sense to discriminate against the young Fascists, first of all because they are "in all ways identical to the majority of their contemporaries. Culturally, psychologically, physically . . . there is nothing to set them apart."[28]

In his attitude of openness toward another kind of "diversity" Pasolini goes even further and upsets firmly consecrated positions: ". . . in reality we behaved with the Fascists (I am speaking mainly of the young ones) in a racist manner: that is, we hastily and ruthlessly wanted to believe that they were racially predestined to be Fascists. . . . But none of us has ever talked with them. We quickly accepted them as inevitable representatives of Evil. . . ."[29]

The young Fascist with whom the poet "talks" in "Saluto e augurio" also assumes the characteristics of a new and problematical alter ego. In a moment when Pasolini is intuitively aware of that part of himself that is gray and reactionary (the part that defends, preserves, and prays) and of his relationship with it, the poetic self seems to split and the dialogue starts: ". . . and I want to talk to a Fascist, before I, or he, gets too far away. . . ."[30]

In light of his past as an intellectual actively, if polemically, on the Left, the poet's attitude toward this part of himself is ambivalent. He tries at times to deny and repudiate it, joining with that same chorus of accusations against Fascism that he has just challenged: "But remember, I have no illusions about you: I know, I know very well that you don't have, and don't want to have, a free heart, and you can't be sincere: but even if you are a dead man, I shall talk to you. . . ."[31]

In this last declaration lies the significance of the poem: Pasolini cannot and will not carry through with the consequences of provocation and scandal. At the end, in fact, he disassociates himself from his alter ego, in a last attempt to overturn the roles and recover his beloved self, young and vital, perennially searching for new values and new myths. His real weariness and disillusionment, his inability to suggest alternatives ("Libro senza la Parola"—Book without the Word)[32] are symbolically unloaded onto the shoulders of an interlocutor—really too different a projection from himself and his past for the identification to be complete: "*Hic desinit cantus.* Take it yourself, this burden, on your shoulders. I cannot. No one would understand the scandal."[33]

What might seem to be the renouncing of an act of provocation ("An old man has respect for the judgment of the world: even if it does not matter to him in the least . . ."[34] in the name of a wise, mature abstention from controversy ("And he has respect for what is in the world . . .")[35] really hides the poet's inability to repress the myth of regression and vitality, in the name of the eternal lad who runs lightly: "Take it yourself, this weight. . . . And I shall walk lightly going forward, choosing for ever life and youth."[36]

As we have noted, Pasolini had already stubbornly denied both his age as regards the myth and his spiritual death, willing to project them onto the outside world—as in "Li litanís del biel fi" (It is not I who am old, but the world that is old. . . .)[37] or in another of the compositions in *Tetro entusiasmo* ("I weep for a dead world. But I who weep am not dead. . . .")[38]

Within the bleak, desperate nihilism of the author's last works, we can interpret his conclusion of the closing poem as an opening to hope.

The fact remains that the opposites are not reconciled even in the poetic testament, and the last two intensely human protagonists embody and seal the extreme unresolved contradiction.

Notes and References

Preface

1. See Franco Fortini, *Saggi italiani* (Bari: De Donato, 1974), pp. 122-23. Following Fortini, Giampaolo Borghello states that: "Under the sign of the synchysis we can then re-read all the works of Pasolini, linking their most diverse aspects . . ., bringing back to *unity*—an open and even dialectical unity—the sparse fragments of an experience giddily extending in all directions."

2. On first reading, a collection of Pasolini's essays based on the psychoanalytic critical approach, published in May, 1979 under the title *Descrizioni di Descrizioni* [Descriptions of Descriptions], seems to confirm my impression.

3. See *Orgia,* note 15.

Chapter One

1. P. P. Pasolini, "Al lettore nuovo," in Pasolini, *Poesie* (Milano, 1970), pp. 6-11.

2. Pasolini, "Appunti *en poète* per una linguistica marxista." Now in Pasolini, *Empirismo Eretico* (Milano, 1972), pp. 62-63, 71-74.

3. Pasolini, *Lettere agli amici* (1941–1945), edited by Luciano Serra (Milano, 1976); also Pasolini, "Lettere a Franco Farolfi," published in *Nuovi Argomenti* (Jan.-March, 1976), p. 3–35.

4. Pasolini, *Lettere agli amici,* p. 6.

5. *Pasolini e "Il Setaccio,"* edited by Mario Ricci (Bologna, 1977), pp. 79-81.

6. Pasolini, *Lettere agli amici,* p. 33.

7. Pasolini, *Passione e ideologia* (Milano, 1973), p. 487.

8. Pasolini, *Lettere agli amici,* p. 43–49.

9. Pasolini, *La religione del mio tempo* (Milano, 1961), p. 54.

10. Pasolini, *La meglio gioventù,* "El Testament Coran." Now in *La nuova gioventù* (Torino, 1975), p. 119.

11. Pasolini, *Lettere agli amici,* p. 43–49.

12. Pasolini, "Al lettore nuovo," in *Poesie,* p. 10. Antonio Gramsci (1891-1927) was a leading Marxist philosopher and literary critic.

13. Pasolini, *Lettere agli amici,* XXIV.

14. Bandini et al., *Pasolini: cronaca giudiziaria, persecuzione, morte* (Milano, 1977), p. 37.

15. Ibid., p. 50.

16. In his *Entretiens avec Pier Paolo Pasolini* (Paris: Pierre Belfond, 1970), p. 113, Jean Duflot posed the following question to the poet: "L'obsession de l'exclusion, de la marginalité, correspond-elle à une expérience douloureusement vécue par vous-même?"

The answer gives the most direct and poignant account of Pasolini's own feeling on "being different": "Cela ne fait aucun doute. Quand je vous dis que j'ai la mentalité d'un animal bléssé, à la traîte de la bande, je vous dis la vérité. . . . La plupart de mes ennuis, la plus grande partie de la haine qui m'est vouée viennent de ce que je suis différent. Je la sens, cette haine, elle est 'raciale'. C'est le racisme que l'on exerce contre toutes les minorités du monde."

17. *Pasolini: cronaca giudiziaria, persecuzione, morte,* p. 52–53.

18. Umberto Eco, "Perché non sempre eravamo d'accordo," in *L'Espresso,* Nov. 9, 1975, p. 11.

Chapter Two

1. *La Fiera Letteraria,* June 30, 1957.

2. Pasolini, *La meglio gioventù,* now in *La nuova gioventù,* op. cit. , p. 153.

3. The title of this early novel is significantly taken from a letter that Marx addressed to Arnold Ruge: "Our goal thus should be the reformation of conscience. . . . It would then be manifest that the world has had for a long time the dream of a thing."

4. Alberto Asor Rosa, *Scrittori e popolo* (Perugia, 1969), p. 370.

5. Pasolini, *Le Ceneri di Gramsci* (Milano, 1957), p. 77.

6. Ibid., pp. 107-8.

7. Georg Lukács's works *The Theory of the Novel* and *The Historical Novel,* and the concern they express with the interaction of time (seen as concrete, historical medium) and prose narrative, heavily influenced Italian literary criticism in the late 1950s.

8. *Ritratti su misura,* edited by Elio F. Accrocca (Venezia: Sodalizio del libro, 1960), p. 321.

9. Pasolini, *La religione del mio tempo* (Milano, 1961), p. 166.

10. Ibid., pp. 158-59.

11. *Pasolini on Pasolini,* Interview with Oswald Stack (London, 1969), pp. 28-29.

12. Ibid., p. 29.
13. Pasolini, *La religione del mio tempo,* p. 46.
14. Pasolini, *Poesia in forma di Rosa* (Milano, 1964), p. 42.
15. The English distributors introduced "St." into the title, against Pasolini's express wish.
16. *Pasolini on Pasolini,* pp. 75 and 97.
17. The essay "Il cinema di poesia" originally published in the review *Film critica,* April-May, 1965, is included in: Pasolini, *Empirismo eretico,* pp. 171-91.
18. From an interview to *Cahiers du Cinéma,* 1969, p. 212.
19. The poem-pamphlet "Il PCI ai giovani," was successively published in *Nuovi Argomenti,* n. 10, April-June, 1968. Now included in Pasolini, *Empirismo eretico,* pp. 155-60, followed by the author's own commentary, "Apologia," pp. 160-63.
20. In *Pasolini on Pasolini,* p. 143, we read: "I wrote some texts for the theater, but I don't know why I wrote them in the first place. . . . The point is that I had not written any poetry for several years, and then suddenly I started again, but for the theater, and in fact I've never written with such ease as I have done for the theater, and nothing has ever been such fun."
21. Pasolini, "La parola orale meravigliosa possibilità del cinema" in *Cinema nuovo,* no. 201, Sept-Oct, 1969, No. 201.
22. Ibid.
23. Sergio Arecco, Pasolini [interview] (Roma: Partisan, 1972), quoted in Vincenzo Mannino, *Invito alla lettura di Pasolini* (Milano, 1974), pp. 50-51.
24. Duflot, Jean, *Entretiens avec Pier Paolo Pasolini* (Paris, 1970), p. 65: "D'ailleurs le prochain ouvrage de poésie que je publierai s'intitulera *Trasumanar e organisar.* Je veux dire par là que l'autre face de la 'transhumanisation' . . . ou de l'ascèse spirituelle, c'est précisément l''organisation' . . ."
25. Pasolini, *Trasumanar e organizzar* (Milano, 1971), pp. 167-68.
26. Pasolini, *Calderón* (Milano, 1973), p. 183.
27. Ibid., p. 176.
28. Pasolini, *Trasumanar e organizzar,* pp. 125-30.
29. In his interview with Sergio Arecco quoted above, Pasolini introduced the meaning and the title of *Empirismo eretico:* "This 'hope' of Marxist praxis and bourgeois pragmatics—where does it come from? It comes from a common source—Hegel. I am *against Hegel* (existentially—heretical empiricism)." See note 23.
30. Pasolini, *Scritti corsari* (Milano, 1975), pp. 111-17.
31. Pasolini, *La nuova gioventù,* p. 193.

32. Ibid., pp. 236-37.

33. The essay "Abiura dalla *Trilogia della vita*" was first published in *Trilogia della vita,* edited by Giorgio Gattei (Bologna, 1975), pp. 11-13. Also published in "Corriere della sera," June 5, 1975, is now included in Pasolini, *Lettere luterane* (Torino, 1976), pp. 71-76.

34. Ibid., pp. 75-76. The word "Salò?" appears in italics in the text.

35. Goethe, J.W., *Faust,* part two, Act V, 12110-11: ". . . The Eternal-Feminine/ Draws us onward."

Chapter Three

1. *Mamma Roma,* ovvero dalla responsabilità individuale alla responsabilità collettiva ("*Mamma Roma,* or from individual to collective responsibility"): "Conversation" edited by Nino Ferrera, *Filmcritica,* Sept., 1962. The reference to the Kindu slaughter of 1962 is clear.

2. Pasolini, *Il padre selvaggio* (Torino, 1975), pp. 60-61. (Italics in the text.) In his *Vita di Pasolini* (Milano, 1978), p. 47, Enzo Siciliano lucidly comments on these verses: "The conflict between father and son . . . has not ceased: even dead his father goes back to incarnate himself in those repressive forms of life that do not allow the truth to be proclaimed. The father is he who tyrannically wants . . . to reestablish 'old truths.' They are degraded truths, to be refused, torn: truths that history has turned, or is about to turn, into lies. Life is elsewhere. . . ."

3. Pasolini, *Poesia in forma di rosa,* p. 208.

4. "La volontà di Dante a essere poeta," written in 1965, included in Pasolini, *Empirismo eretico,* p. 109.

5. Pasolini, *La Divina Mimesis* (Torino, 1975), p. 6.

6. Ibid.

7. The week of May 22-28, 1968 is that of the "students revolution" in Rome.

8. Siciliano, *Vita di Pasolini,* pp. 76-77.

9. Pasolini, *I Turcs tal Friûl* (Udine, 1976), p. 76.

10. Ibid., p. 34.

Chapter Four

1. The dates indicated by Pasolini are those of the composition of the various groups.

2. Giuliano Manacorda, *Storia della letteratura italiana contemporanea 1940–1965* (Roma, 1967), p. 254.

3. Pasolini, "La poesia dialettale–Il Friuli" (1952). Now in *Passione e Ideologia,* p. 137.

4. Pasolini, *Empirismo eretico,* p. 62-63. (Italics in the text.)
5. Giorgio Caproni, "Appunti" in *Paragone Letteratura,* Feb., 1955, p. 84.
6. Pasolini, *La nuova gioventù* (Torino, 1975). (Including all the poems of *La meglio gioventù.*) All subsequent references are to this edition. Note on p. 157.
7. Ibid.
8. Ibid., p. 8. I follow Pasolini's version in rhythmic prose.
9. Ibid.
10. Ibid., p. 11.
11. Ibid., p. 16.
12. Ibid., p. 53.
13. Ibid., p. 55.
14. Ibid., p. 153.
15. Ibid., p. 101.
16. Ibid., p. 129.
17. Ibid., p. 11.
18. Ibid., p. 7.
19. Ibid., p. 167.
20. Ibid., p. 20.
21. Ibid., p. 188.
22. Ibid., p. 18.
23. Ibid., p. 19.
24. Ibid., p. 54.
25. Ibid., p. 53.
26. Ibid., p. 35.
27. Ibid., p. 60.
28. Ibid., p. 80.
29, Ibid., p. 173.
30. Ibid., p. 187.
31. As quoted by Luise Vinge, in *The Narcissus Theme in Western European Literature up to the Early Nineteenth Century,* translated by Robert Dewsnap (Lund: Gleerups, 1967):

> Quod petis, est nusquam; quod amas, avertere, perdes!
> Ista repercussae, quam cernis, imaginis umbra est:
> Nil habet ista sui: tecum venitque manetque,
> Tecum discedet, si tu discedere possis.

P. Ovidius Naso, Vol. II, *Metamorphoses,* editio major, Rudolf Ehewald, ed. (Leipzig, 1915), v.v. 433-36.

Chapter Five

1. The theoretical assumptions underlying the proposal of a linguistic agglomerate exemplified in the two Roman novels have been fully elaborated by Pasolini in several of the essays now included in *Passione e Ideologia.* See "Il Reame" (especially pp. 11-13); "Gadda: Le novelle dal Ducato in fiamme" (pp. 313-14); and "La libertà stilistica" (pp. 486-87). In these essays the author interprets, in a political and sociological key, the opposition (traditionally relegated to the historical-linguistic sphere) between cultivated, academic Italian and plurilinguism.

2. Pasolini, *The ragazzi,* translated by Emile Capouya (New York: Grove Press, Inc., 1968), p. 119. The following is the original version of the paragraph quoted from Pasolini, *Ragazzi di vita* (Milano, 1955), p. 113:

. . . Il fratello dormiva come una cucuzza, con la bocca mezza aperta e le lenzuola intorcinate tra le gambe, ma dopo un po' cominciò a dare segni di fastidio: e si rivoltò di colpo, portandosi tutte le lenzuola sotto la pancia. Il Lenzetta, ubbriaco fracico, continuò a cantare a tutto gasse. L'altro allora si svegliò di botto e fece: "Aòh?" "Vaffan . . ." rispose il Lenzetta alzandosi in piedi. Il fratello si rese conto di ciò che succedeva, lo guardò, gli diede una spinta che lo spiccicò contro il muro e si riappennicò.

In his recent "Vita di Pasolini," cited above, Enzo Siciliano (pp. 188, 189-90) provides us attestations which, if on the one hand add to the problematic aspect of the linguistic solutions of *Ragazzi di vita* and its historical and philological "legitimacy," on the other hand are fundamental for the total interpretation of the poet's works:

Is the "Romanesco" dialect in which the novel was written philologically arbitrary? Among the boys he met in the slum, Pasolini found a "consultant," Sergio Citti—"my living lexicon of Romanesco," he called him. . . . It was the summer of 1951. Pier Paolo saw Citti for the first time on the bed of the Aniene river near the Mammolo bridge. . . . Sergio was eighteen years old, and had left the reformatory a few weeks before . . . Pier Paolo said that he was writing a book about the slum boys and asked for Sergio's help. Pasolini and Citti started getting together. . . . Pasolini had a notebook open in front of him: he asked Sergio for precise linguistic data with the obstinate, quibbling manner of the professional linguist . . . So, was the Roman dialect that Sergio suggested totally arbitrary? It was a jargon within a jargon:—gang slang, invented to encode the communication between friends . . . but also a jargon testifying to a tragic ghetto, to a sickened, marginal humanity.

Pasolini was too good a philologist to deny himself this experience, and its poetic reinvention. The "subjectivity" of this language turned irresistably to "objectivity" . . . Thus that jargon lost some of its merely literary finality: it was used for purely cognitive ends. . . . It changed . . . into a language whose function was to exalt, to define the opposition between one universe, one hell, and the rest of the universe.

3. Pasolini, *The Ragazzi,* translated by Emile Capouya, p. 43. Original text from Pasolini, *Ragazzi di vita,* p. 36, follows:

Era una bella mattina, col sole che ardeva, libero e giocondo, battendo sui Grattacieli puliti, freschi, attraverso chilometri d'azzurro, e facendo piovere oro da tutte le parti. Sulle gobbe riverniciate del Monte di Splendore o di Casadio, sulle facciate dei palazzoni, sui cortili interni, sui marciapiedi: e in mezzo a tutto quell'oro e a quella freschezza, la gente vestita a festa formicolava al centro di Donna Olimpia, alle porte dei caseggiati, intorno al chiosco del giornalaio . . .

4. Pasolini, *The Ragazzi,* translated by Emile Capouya, p. 136.

Chapter Six

1. Pasolini, *Poesie* (Milano, 1970). "Al lettore nuovo" [To the new reader], preface, pp. 6-11.
2. Pasolini, *Le Ceneri di Gramsci* (Milano, 1957), p. 15. All subsequent references are to this edition. All translations are mine.

Un esercito accampato nell'attesa
di farsi cristiano nella cristiana
città, occupa una marcita distesa

d'erba sozza nell'accesa campagna:
scendere anch'egli dentro la borghese
luce spera aspettando una umana

abitazione, esso, sardo o pugliese,
dentro un porcile il fangoso desco
in villaggi ciechi tra lucide chiese

novecentesche e grattacieli.

3. Ibid., pp. 23-24:

> Ragazzo del popolo che canti,
> qui a Rebibbia sulla misera riva
> dell'Aniene la nuova canzonetta, vanti
> é vero, cantando, l'antica, la festiva
> leggerezza dei semplici. Ma quale
> dura certezza tu sollevi insieme
> d'imminente riscossa, in mezzo a ignari
> tuguri e grattacieli, allegro seme
> in cuore al triste mondo popolare?

4. "L'umile Italia" does not immediately follow "Il Canto popolare" in the collection, but it is, in my opinion, closely connected to the first two poems. Ibid., p. 55:

> E necessità il capire
> e il fare: il credersi volti
> al meglio, presi da un ardire
> sacrilego a scordare i morti,
> a non concedersi respiro
> dietro il rinnovarsi del tempo.

5. Ibid., p. 34:

> . . . Nel restare
> dentro l'inferno con marmorea
>
> volontà di capirlo, è da cercare
> la salvezza.

6. Ibid., pp. 42 and 44:

> . . . Non è l'aspetto
>
> di gente viva con me, questo, nei
> suoi visi c'è un tempo morto che torna
> inaspettato, odioso, quasi i bei

giorni della vittoria, i freschi giorni
del popolo, fossero essi, morti.

. . . Egli chiede pietà, con quel suo modesto,
tremendo sguardo, non per il suo destino,
ma per il nostro . . . Ed è lui, il troppo onesto,
il troppo puro, che deve andare a capo chino?

7. In the "Notes" following the poems, and under "Le Ceneri di Gramsci," Pasolini writes: "Gramsci is buried in a small grave in the English Cemetery, between Porta San Paolo and Testaccio [in Rome], not far from Shelley's grave. On the tombstone the only words are: 'Cinera Gramsci,' and the dates." Ibid., p. 142.

8. Ibid., pp. 76-77:

. . . sussisto

perchè non scelgo. Vivo nel non volere
del tramontato dopoguerra: amando
il mondo che odio—nella sua miseria

sprezzante e perso—per un oscuro scandalo
della conscienza . . .

Lo scandalo del contraddirmi, dell'essere
con te e contro te; con te nel cuore,
in luce, contro te nelle buie viscere;

9. See note 1, Preface.

10. *Interpretazioni di Pasolini,* edited by Giampaolo Borghello (Roma, 1977), p. 21.

11. Pasolini, *Le Ceneri,* p. 73:

Nei cerchi dei sarcofaghi non fanno

che mostrare la superstite sorte
di gente laica le laiche iscrizioni
in queste grige pietre, corte

e imponenti. Ancora di passioni
sfrenate senza scandalo son arse
le ossa dei miliardari di nazioni

più grandi; ronzano, quasi mai scomparse,
le ironie dei principi, dei pederasti,

. . . Qui il silenzio della morte è fede
di un civile silenzio di uomini rimasti
uomini, . . .

12. Ibid.:

grassa di ortiche e di legumi dà
questi magri cipressi, . . .

13. Alberto Asor Rosa, *Scrittori e popolo* (Perugia, 1965), p. 406.
14. Gian Carlo Ferretti, *Letteratura e ideologia* (Roma, 1964), p. 281.
15. Pasolini, *Le Ceneri,* p. 118:

. . . Piange ciò che ha
fine e ricomincia. Ciò che era
area erbosa, aperto spiazzo, e si fa
cortile, bianco come cera,

. . . e si fa nuovo isolato, brulicante
in un ordine ch'è spento dolore.

Piange ciò che muta, anche
per farsi migliore. . . .

16. Ibid., p. 114:

. . . Ecco, se acceso
alle speranza—che, vecchio leone
puzzolente di vodka, dall'offesa

sua Russia giura Krusciov al mondo
ecco che tu ti accorgi che sogni.
Sembra bruciare nel felice agosto

di pace, ogni tua passione, ogni
tuo interiore tormento,
ogni tua ingenua vergogna

di non essere—nel sentimento—
al punto in cui il mondo si rinnova.

17. Ferretti, *Letteratura e ideologia,* p. 289.
18. Pasolini, *Le Ceneri,* p. 122.
19. Ibid., pp. 124-25:

. . . ma il vostro dolore
di non esserne più sul primo fronte,
sarebbe più puro, se nell'ora

in cui l'errore, anche se puro, si sconta,
aveste la forza di dirvi colpevoli. . . .

. . . vi siete assuefatti,
voi, servi della giustizia, leve

della speranza, ai necessari atti
che umiliano il cuore e la coscienza.

. . . Avete, accecati dal fare, servito
il popolo non nel suo cuore

ma nella sua bandiera; . . .

20. Ibid., p. 127:

. . . Snodati i ragazzi
dentro i panni festivi, ricchi

di nastri, fazzoletti, sono come pazzi
di pregustata gioia sotta i cappelli
messicani, rossi come sangue, e tra spiazzi

e albereti, si muovono in drappelli
disordinati, in branchi, soli,
masticando gomma americana, nella

loro generosità senza pudore.

21. Ibid.:

Gli uomini, già perduti in un'abbietta
ubriachezza, nascosta come un dolore,

si portano dietro la famiglia, stretta
intorno alla sporta della merenda,

22. Ibid., pp. 128-29:

Ed ecco, incerto, un vecchio si leva
dalla testa bianca il berretto,

afferra nella nuova ventata di passione
una bandiera retta sulle spalle
da uno che gli è davanti, al petto

se la stringe, . . .

. . . Poi il canto, che s'era levato
gioioso, disperato, cessa, e il vecchio

lascia cadere la bandiera, e lento,
con le lacrime agli occhi,
si ricalca in capo il suo berretto.

23. Leonardo Sciascia (a careful reader of Pasolini) has given, in a page which I consider to be inspired by the poems written by Pasolini in 1956, a restatement of that distressing sense of the inadequacy of institutionalized

Marxist interpretational schemas, and of the mystification that formulas and dogmas brought about, affecting the "people" in the Party. The reference to Sciascia's words is useful because they clarify and reaffirm, twenty years later, Pasolini's position.

Sciascia's *Candido* (Torino: Einandi, 1977), p. 85, The text follows:

> . . . peasants, workers, miners: real people, down to earth, who spoke of their own needs and those of the city in few words and to the point; sometimes summing up a whole argument in a single proverb. And there was quite a clear contrast, even if no one noticed it, between the ones who, by number, need, and hope made up a party, and those whom the party represented and led: the unaccountable and elusive arguments of the former; the interjections, rapid and dry like target shots, of the latter, not without, at times, pointed irony.
>
> Don Antonio saw in this contrast, which never came out in the open, a repetition of what happened, and had always happened, in the Church. . . .
>
> The leaders of the Party still, therefore, talked to the souls of people who only could—and only knew how to—talk of their bodies.

24. Pasolini, *Le Ceneri,* p. 136:

> Sono sempre stati per loro unica legge
> odio servile e servile allegria: eppure
> nei loro occhi si poteva leggere
>
> ormai un segno di diversa fame—scura
> come quella del pane, e, come
> quella, necessaria. Una pura
>
> ombra che già prendeva nome
> di speranza: . . .

25. Asor Rosa, *Scrittori e popolo,* p. 376.
26. Pasolini, *Le Ceneri,* p. 138:

> Tu ti perdi nel paradiso interiore,
> e anche la tua pietà gli è nemica.

27. Pasolini, *Passione e ideologia* (Milano, 1960), p. 487.

28. Ibid., pp. 487-88.
29. Ibid., p. 489 (Italics in the text).
30. Edoardo Sanguineti, *Ideologia e linguaggio* (Milano: Feltrinelli, 1965), p. 11.
31. Ibid., p. 14.
32. Cesare Garboli, *La stanza separata* (Milano: Mondadori, 1969), p. 17.
33. In the quotations, the following abbreviations are used:

P.V. = "Una polemica in versi"
C.G. = "Le Ceneri di Gramsci"
P.S. = "Il pianto della scavatrice"

All quotations are from Pasolini, *Le Ceneri.*

Chapter Seven

1. Pier Paolo Pasolini, *Teorema* (Milano, 1968), pp. 10-11.
2. Ibid., p. 12.
3. Ibid., p. 16.
4. Ibid., p. 19.
5. Ibid., p. 20.
6. Ibid., p. 23-24.
7. Ibid., p. 195.
8. Gian Carlo Ferretti, *Pasolini: l'universo orrendo* (Roma, 1976), p. 64.
9. Pasolini, *Teorema,* p. 5.
10. Ibid., p. 88.
11. Ibid., p. 204.
12. The following are the "corollaries" that in the second part of *Teorema* refer to Odetta, Pietro, and Lucia:
    4. "Where it says how Odetta ended up losing or betraying God."
    11. "Where it says how young master Pietro ended up losing or betraying God."
    13. "Where it says how Lucia also ended up losing or betraying God."
13. Pasolini, *Teorema,* p. 200.
14. Ibid., pp. 98-99.
15. Ibid., p. 146.
16. Ibid., p. 100.
17. Ibid., pp. 103-4.

18. The quotation, introduced by Pasolini simply as "From A. Rimbaud's *Poésies,*" is taken from the poem "Les Soeurs de Charité." (See *Oeuvres de Rimbaud,* Edition de Suzanne Bernard, Paris: Garnier, 1969, p. 108).

Pasolini, *Teorema,* p. 203:

> Le jeune homme dont l'oeil est brillant, la peau brune,
> Le beau corps de vingt ans qui devrait aller nu,
> Et qu'eût, le front cerclé de cuivre, sous la lune
> Adoré, dans la Perse, un Génie inconnu,
> Impétueux avec des douceurs virginales
> Et noires, fier de ses premiers entêtements,
> Pareils aux jeunes mers. . .
>
> (Da "Poésies" di A. Rimbaud)

19. See *Oeuvres de Rimbaud,* p. 188.
20. Rimbaud, *Les Illuminations,* III, "Coute." See Rimbaud, *Une saison en Enfer, Les Illuminations,* A new translation by Rhodes Peschel Endi, (New York: Oxford University Press, 1973), p. 117.
21. Ibid., p. 127: X, "To a Reason" and p. 171: XL, "Génie."
22. Tommaso Anzoino, *Pasolini* (Firenze, 1971), p. 2.
23. Ibid., pp. 69-70.
24. Michel David, *La psicoanalisi nella cultura italiana* (Torino: Boringhieri, 1966), p. 559.
25. Pasolini, *Teorema,* p. 25.
26. Ibid., p. 32.
27. Ibid., p. 131.
28. Ibid., pp. 9-10.

Chapter Eight

1. Gualtiero De Santi, "Il teatro di parola." In *Perchè Pasolini,* Gualtiero De Santi et al. (Firenze, 1978), p. 79.
2. Pasolini, "Manifesto per un nuovo teatro." First published in *Nuovi argomenti* n. 9, January, March, 1968. All references are made to the edition of the "Manifesto" published in *I quaderni del Teatro Stabile della Città di Torino,* n. 13, 1968.
3. Pasolini, "Manifesto," p. 55, clause 20, b.
4. Ibid., p. 47, clause 7.
5. Ibid., p. 48, clause 8. Italics in the text.
6. Ibid., p. 47, clause 3.
7. Ibid., p. 52, clause 17.
8. De Santi, op. cit., p. 88.

9. Pasolini, "A teatro con Pasolini," *Il Giorno,* December 1, 1968. (For the sake of readability I have eliminated some of the quotation marks of the original.)

10. De Santi, p. 89.

11. Siciliano, *Vita di Pasolini* (Milano, 1978), p. 298.

12. To this day there has not yet been published a critical edition of Pasolini's theatrical works. I am indebted to the direction of the Teatro Stabile [Resident Theater] of the city of Torino for a photostatic copy of *Orgia,* complete with corrections by the hand of the author. All references are made to this copy.*

13. Pasolini, *Orgia,* episode 1.

14. Ibid., episode 6. (It is important to notice the consistency of this monologue and of the entire sixth episode, with *Teorema,* especially with Pietro's appendix, "Sete di morte"; Pasolini, *Teorema,* p. 97.) Italics in the text.

15. Pasolini, *Orgia,* episode 1.

* *Orgia* was published, with *Porcile,* in 1979. See bibliography.

Chapter Nine

1. Pasolini, *Lettere luterane* (Torino: 1976), p. 73. Italics in the text.

2. Ferretti, *L'Universo Orrendo* (Roma, 1976), p. 105.

3. See Pasolini, *La nuova gioventù,* p. 264, note: " 'Tetro entusiasmo' is an expression taken from Dostoevskiy's [*sic*] *Crime and Punishment.*"

In the introductory note, on pages 5 and 6 of *Scritti corsari* referring to the two parts of the volume, the poet writes: "The reconstruction of this book is entrusted to the reader. . . . It is he who must reunite distant passages that are, however, related. It is he who must organize the contradictory moments, seeking out their substantial wholeness. . . . This work that the reader must reconstruct lacks even some of the basic materials. I refer specifically to a group of Italo-Friulian poems that constitute an essential nexus, not only between the two 'series' but also within the first 'series' itself. . . . Therefore the reader is referred to them."

4. Pasolini, *La nuova gioventù,* p. 189.

5. Ibid., p. 251.

6. Ibid., p. 234.

7. Pasolini, *Scritti corsari,* "Jan. 7, 1973: A 'disquisition' on hair," pp. 14-15.

8. Pasolini, *La nuova gioventù,* p. 245.

9. Ibid., p. 244.

10. Ibid., p. 259.

11. Ibid., p. 256.

12. One may speak with Ferretti of a personal "relaunching" of the poet and the reassembling within his discourse "of a real and diffused interest, problematical and controversial, both on the part of intellectuals and politicians, and on the part of a vast youthful public (and among his readers Pasolini will also find not a few of those students of '68, whose inability and impossibility of understanding him he had substantially theorized) . . ." Ferretti, *L'Universo orrendo,* p. 86.

13. Pasolini, *La nuova gioventù,* p. 257.

14. Ibid., p. 256-57.

15. Ibid., p. 257.

16. "The world is the reality that you have always paternally wanted." Pasolini, *Il padre selvaggio* (Torino, 1975), p. 61.

17. Pasolini, *La nuova gioventù,* p. 257.

18. Ibid., p. 258.

19. Ibid., p.257.

20. Pasolini, *Scritti corsari,* "May 17, 1973. Linguistic analysis of a slogan," p. 20.

21. Ibid., pp. 17-23. The article quoted in note 20 was first published in "Corriere della sera," with the title "The insane slogan of 'Jesus' jeans," and it referred to a notorious slogan: "Jesus jeans: thou shall have no other jeans besides myself."

22. Pasolini, *Scritti corsari,* p. 101.

23. Pasolini, *La nuova gioventù,* p. 258.

24. Ibid., p. 258-59.

25. Pasolini, *Scritti corsari,* pp. 25-26.

26. Ibid., p. 289-90.

27. Pasolini further elaborates this point in his review of Sandro Penna's novel *Un po' di febbre.* In *Scritti Corsari,* pp. 179-84.

28. Ibid., p. 54-55.

29. Ibid., p. 62.

30. Pasolini, *La nuova gioventù,* p. 255.

31. Ibid., p. 256.

32. Ibid., p. 259.

33. Ibid.

34. Ibid.

35. Ibid.

36. Ibid.

37. Ibid., p. 173.

38. Ibid., p. 237.

Selected Bibliography

PRIMARY SOURCES

The first edition of each work is listed. When I have not used the first edition, I have indicated in the Notes the particular edition used. Only Pasolini's books are noted here. Whenever one of the author's articles, contributions, or interviews is cited in the text, the corresponding reference appears in the Notes.

POETRY

Le ceneri di Gramsci. Milano: Garzanti, 1957.
Dal Diario. Caltanissetta: Sciascia, 1954.
La meglio gioventù. Firenze: Sansoni, 1954.
La nuova gioventù. Torino: Einaudi, 1975.
Poesia in forma di rosa. Milano: Garzanti, 1964.
Poesie (An anthology of poems selected by the author). Milano: Garzanti, 1970.
La religione del mio tempo. Milano: Garzanti, 1961.
Roma 1950. Diario. Milano: Scheiwiller, 1960.
Sonetto primaverile. Milano: Scheiwiller, 1960.
Trasumanar e organizzar. Milano: Garzanti, 1971.
L'Usignolo della Chiesa cattolica. Milano: Longanesi, 1958 (now also in: Torino: Einaudi, 1976).

NARRATIVE

Alì dagli occhi azzurri. Milano: Garzanti, 1965.
La Divina Mimesis. Torino: Einaudi, 1975.
Il padre selvaggio. Torino: Einaudi, 1975.
Ragazzi di vita. Milano: Garzanti, 1955.

San Paolo. Torino: Einaudi, 1977.
Il sogno di una cosa. Milano: Garzanti, 1962.
Teorema. Milano: Garzanti, 1968.
Una vita violenta. Milano: Garzanti, 1959.

ESSAYS

Canzoniere italiano. Antologia della poesia popolare. Parma: Guanda, 1955.
Descrizioni di Descrizioni. Torino: Einaudi, 1979.
Empirismo eretico. Milano: Garzanti, 1972.
Lettere luterane. Torino: Einaudi, 1976.
"*Manifesto per un nuovo teatro.*" *Nuovi Argomenti,* n. 9, January, March, 1968.
L'odore dell'India. Milano: Garzanti, 1962.
Passione e ideologia. Milano: Garzanti, 1960.
Poesia dialettale del Novecento (in cooperation with Mario dell'Arco). Parma: Guanda, 1952.
La poesia popolare italiana. Milano: Garzanti, 1960.
Scritti corsari. Milano: Garzanti, 1975.

SCRIPTS

Accattone. Roma: FM, 1961.
Edipo Re. Milano: Garzanti, 1970.
Mamma Roma. Milano: Rizzoli, 1962.
Medea. Milano: Garzanti, 1970.
Trilogia della vita (Decameron, I racconti di Canterbury, Il fiore delle Mille e una notte). Bologna: Cappeli, 1975.
Uccellacci e uccellini. Milano: Garzanti, 1965.
Il Vangelo secondo Matteo. Milano: Garzanti, 1964.

THEATER

Affabulazione Pilade. Milano: Garzanti, 1977.
Calderón. Milano: Garzanti, 1973.
Porcile, Orgia. Milano: Garzanti, 1979.
I Turcs tal Friúl. Udine: Forum Julii, 1976.

TRANSLATION

Il Vantone. Milano: Garzanti, 1963.

MISCELLANEOUS

Le belle bandiere. Dialogues 1960-65. Edited by Gian Carlo Ferretti. Roma: Editori Riuniti, 1977.
I disegni, 1941, 75. Edited by Giuseppe Zigaina. Milano: Scheiwiller, 1978.
Lettere agli amici (1941-1945). Edited by Luciano Serra. Milano: Guanda, 1976.
Pasolini e "Il Setaccio," 1942-43. Edited by Mario Ricci. Bologna: Cappelli, 1977.

FILMS

Accattone, 1961.
Appunti per un film sull'India, 1969.
Appunti per una Orestiade africana, 1969.
Che cosa sono le nuvole (an episode of *Capriccio all'italiana*), 1967.
Comizi d'amore, 1964.
Edipo re, 1967.
12 dicembre, 1972.
Il Decameron, 1971
Il fiore delle Mille e una notte, 1974.
Mamma Roma, 1962.
Medea, 1969.
Porcile, 1969.
La ricotta (an episode of *Rogopag*), 1963.
Salò o le 120 giornate di Sodoma, 1975.
La sequenza del fiore di carta (an episode of *Amore e rabbia*), 1968.
Teorema, 1968.
La terra vista dalla luna (an episode of *Le streghe*), 1966.
Uccellacci e uccellini, 1966.

SECONDARY SOURCES

A detailed bibliography of commentaries written on Pier Paolo Pasolini's works up to 1963 was compiled by Gian Carlo Ferretti and published in the "Bibliographic Appendix" to the chapter "La contrastata rivolta di Pasolini," in *Letteratura e ideologia,* pp. 368-75.

Another substantial bibliography of significant essays on Pasolini may be found in *Interpretazioni di Pasolini,* by Giampaolo Borghello. Roma: Savelli, 1977, pp. 31-34.

In Italian

ANZOINO, TOMMASO. *Pasolini.* Firenze: La nuova Italia, 1971. A lucid analysis of the ideological position of Pasolini, stressing the visceral, sentimental character of his Marxism. The chapter on *Alì dagli occhi azzurri* is particularly interesting and detailed.

ASOR ROSA, ALBERTO. *Scrittori e popolo.* Perugia: Samoná e Savelli, 1965. The last chapter of this book, which deals with populist literature in Italy, is dedicated to Pasolini (pp. 349–449). Identifies the highest moment of the poet's career in the central poem of *Le Ceneri di Gramsci.* The rest of Pasolini's production appears to Asor Rosa to be "an aesthetic adventure" developed against the background of the ideological tensions in Italy in the 1950s and early 1960s.

BANDINI, FERNANDO, et al. *Pasolini: Cronaca giudiziaria, persecuzione, morte.* Milano: Garzanti, 1977. A collection of too many, uneven, sometimes perfunctory articles. Very informative introduction by Bandini. Excellent contributions by De Mauro, Fortini, and Scalia. Mario Spinella gives instructive account of Pasolini's early relationship with the Italian Communist Party.

BARBERI-SQUAROTTI, GIORGIO. "Appunti" ("Le Ceneri di Gramsci"), in *Paragone-Letteratura,* June, 1959, pp. 85-90. An exhaustive, perspicacious study of Pasolini's linguistic and metric experimentation.

BORGHELLO, GIAMPAOLO, et al. *Interpretazioni di Pasolini.* Roma: Savelli, 1977. A well-conceived selection of forty-one critical essays on Pasolini's formation and works, introduced by Borghello's valuable commentary.

DE SANTI, GUALTIERO, et al. *Perchè Pasolini. Ideologia e stile di un intellettuale militante.* Firenze: Guaraldi, 1978. A collection of serious essays on Pasolini's ideology and style.

FERRETTI, GIAN CARLO. *Letteratura e ideologia.* Roma: Editori Riuniti, 1964. The second part of this book, entitled "La contrastata rivolta di

Pasolini" (pp. 163-356) analyzes the works published by the poet up to 1963. Identifies the nucleus of Pasolini's poetry in the contrast between the Friulian myth and history. In the last works analyzed (especially *La Religione del mio tempo*) glimpses the symptoms of the crisis of rational and historical tension and the first formulation of the theme of "revolutionary desistance." Stresses the importance of *Accattone* for the understanding of Pasolini's problematics of the sub-proletariat.

———. *L'Universo orrendo.* Roma: Editori Riuniti, 1976. Continues and completes the preceding study, analyzing works from the early Sixties, indicating "the horrendous universe" as the dominant motif of Pasolini's ideology during the last fifteen years of his life. Gives an open unapologetic portrait of the author, drawn with objectivity and a steady, critical perspective.

FORTINI, FRANCO. "Esistenza e manierismo in Pier Paolo Pasolini," in *I poeti del Novecento.* Roma: Laterza, 1977, pp. 179-89. Indicates Pasolini's highest poetic moments in *La meglio gioventù, L'usignolo della chiesa cattolica,* and *Le Ceneri di Gramsci.* Stresses the author's ability to understand and express (sometimes oversimplifying them) the basic historical correlations of our time.

———. "Le poesie italiane di questi anni," in *Menabó,* no. 2, 1960, pp. 130–39, now in FORTINI, F., *Saggi italiani.* Bari: De Donato, 1974, pp. 122-133. Includes a fundamental analysis of the short poem "Il pianto della scavatrice."

GIAMMATTEO (Di) FERNANDO, et al. *Lo scandalo Pasolini.* Roma: Ateneo, 1976. An attempt to present and organize various opinions on the significance of Pasolini's presence within the Italian cultural life of the last twenty years.

Istituto Italiano di Cultura. "Newsletter," March, 1976, pp. 1-8. Dedicated to Pasolini's "life and works."

LAWTON, BEN. "Boccaccio and Pasolini: A Contemporary Reinterpretation of *The Decameron,*" in *The Decameron 21 Novelle, Contemporary Reactions, Modern Criticism.* Selected, translated, and edited by Mark Musa and Peter E. Bondanella. New York: W. W. Norton and Company, 1977. Professor Lawton's essay is one of the most comprehensive and objective analyses I have read so far on Pasolini's cinematographic interpretation of *The Decameron.* It includes a lucid introduction to Pasolini's whole cinematic work.

LAZAGNA, PIETRO and CARLA. *Pasolini di fronte al problema religioso.* Bologna: Dehoniana, 1970. The hypothesis of a superimposition of

Pasolini's advanced Catholicism (open to Marxist values) and his equally advanced Marxism (open to religious values) appears interesting but heavily normative and not clearly verified.

MANACORDA, GIULIANO. *Storia della letteratura italiana contemporanea* (1940–1965). Roma: Editori Riuniti, 1967. In the pages dedicated to Pasolini (254–63) Manacorda too maintains that *Le Ceneri di Gramsci* marks Pasolini's moment of highest poetic achievement.

MANNINO, VINCENZO. *Invito alla lettura di Pasolini.* Milano: Mursia, 1974. In this uneven monograph the awareness of the importance of linguistic and stylistic experimentation in Pasolini's works is particularly interesting.

"Pasolini, un anno dopo." Nuova generazione, no. 15, Oct. 31, 1976. A collection of articles and statements. Includes political (Gianni Borgna, Giovanni Berlinguer, and Fernando Adornato) and cultural (Paolo Volponi) analyses and the penetrating study by Tullio De Mauro on the linguistic aspects of Pasolini's writings, as well as contributions on his theatrical works, cinema, and even paintings. Set up as a comparison and discussion, and therefore without organic rigor, this collection has the indisputable advantage of being up to date.

PETRAGLIA, SANDRO. *Pier Paolo Pasolini.* Firenze: La nuova Italia, 1974. An excellent monograph, focusing primarily on Pasolini's films and early poetry.

SALINARI, CARLO. "La questione del realismo" (1959), now in *Preludio e fine del realismo in Italia.* Napoli: Morano, 1967, pp. 57-63. Defines *Ragazzi di vita* a passive registration of events, and a "naturalistic" novel, giving the term "naturalism" a negative connotation, opposed to "realism".

———. "La sorte del romanzo" (1959), now in *Preludio e fine. . .,* pp. 141-48. Gives a positive evaluation of *Una vita violenta,* redeemed by the presence of a protagonist stylistically concluded and realistically drawn.

SICILIANO, ENZO. *Vita di Pasolini.* Milano: Rizzoli, 1978. The result of a most careful and comprehensive research, introducing biographical evidences never made public before, this intellectual biography also presents a well-founded overall critical view of Pasolini's works.

ZANZOTTO, ANDREA and NALDINI, NICO. *Pasolini. Poesie e pagine ritrovate.* Roma: Lato Side, 1980. A compassionate contribution to Pasolini's biography by the poet's cousin Nico Naldini, followed by a penetrating essay on Pasolini's poetry by Zanzotto.

In English

The Ragazzi. (*Ragazzi di vita*) Translated by Emile Capouya. New York: Grove Press, 1968.

A Violent Life. (*Una vita violenta*) Translated by William Weaver. New York and London: Garland Publishing Inc., 1978.

Few works on Pasolini have been written in English. Two of the more enlightening studies of the problem of the linguistic instrument (verified in *Ragazzi di vita* and *Una vita violenta*), as well as its historical and literary antecedents, are the following:

O'NEILL, THOMAS. "Il filologo come politico: Linguistic Theory and its Source in P. P. Pasolini," in *Italian Studies,* vol. XXV, 1970.

RAGUSA, OLGA. "Gadda, Pasolini and experimentalism: form or ideology?" now in *From verismo to experimentalism; essays on the modern Italian novel.* Bloomington: Indiana University Press, 1969. Especially pp. 242-43 and 256-64. In this study, the origin, elements, and function of the linguistic medium of the two Roman novels are elaborated against the background of a comparison with Gadda. Particularly interesting are the pages dedicated to Pasolini as a reader of Gadda.

STACK, OSWALD. *Pasolini on Pasolini.* London: Thames and Hudson, 1969. While the first chapter, "Background," deals with Pasolini's life and formation, the rest of the volume is a source of first-hand collected attestations on his cinematographic as well as his literary works. The brief bibliography (mainly concerning the films) that concludes the volume is useful, and the interested reader is referred to it.

WILLEMEN, PAUL et al. *Pier Paolo Pasolini.* London: British Film Institute, 1977. Presents a collection of serious studies on Pasolini's film work.

Index